THE DEATH OF GOD

Gabriel Vahanian

THE

DEATH

OF

GOD

The Culture of Our Post-Christian Era

GEORGE BRAZILLER

NEW YORK

Library of Congress Catalog Card Number: 61-9962

Grateful acknowledgment is made:
To E. P. Dutton & Co., Inc. and Curtis Brown, Ltd. for
quotation from JUSTINE of Lawrence Durrell's translation
of seven lines from Cavafy's The City.
To Grove Press, Inc. and Faber and Faber, Ltd. for quotation
from WAITING FOR GODOT by Samuel Beckett. Copyright
1954 by Grove Press.

1. Secularism

2. Civilization, Modern

Acknowledgments

I WISH to take this opportunity to thank all those who—since I borrow or quote from their works—have influenced and shaped my thinking in a manner obvious to the reader: my hope is that this indebtedness to those I cite and sometimes forget to cite is not devious. I also wish to thank those who guided me in the years of my intellectual formation, in particular the late Professor Pierre Maury and Professor Paul Lehmann. My debt to them continues even though fellow students would agree with me that this book is hardly an adequate expression either of what we were taught or of my gratitude.

I am also indebted beyond measure to Professor Paul Ramsey for his painstaking reading of the manuscript and his careful suggestions. I must, however, assume the responsibility for the statements made in this work. Mrs. Marian Maury has rendered me the invaluable service of intelligently editing the final draft.

Acknowledgments

I have incorporated into this book the following material which has appeared elsewhere. I have reproduced almost in its entirety "This Post-Christian Era" (*The Nation,* December 12, 1959) and quoted from the following: "The God We Deserve" (*The Nation,* February 20, 1960); "The Great Whatever" (*The Nation,* March 7, 1959); "Plea for a New Reformation" (*The Nation,* April 16, 1960); "The Empty Cradle" (*Theology Today,* January, 1957). I gladly record here my thanks to the respective publishers of these magazines for permission to make use again of these articles.

When Zarathustra was alone he said to his heart: "Could it be possible! This old saint in the forest hath not yet heard of it, that God is dead!"

THUS SPAKE ZARATHUSTRA
Friedrich Nietzsche

To kill God is to become god oneself; it is to realize already on this earth the eternal life of which the Gospel speaks.

THE MYTH OF SISYPHUS
Albert Camus

The god that can be pointed out is an idol, and the religiosity that makes an outward show is an imperfect form of religiosity.

CONCLUDING UNSCIENTIFIC POSTSCRIPT
Søren Kierkegaard

The most dreadful sort of blasphemy is that of which "Christendom" is guilty: transforming the God of Spirit into . . . ludicrous twaddle. And the stupidest divine worship, more stupid than anything that is or was to be found in paganism, more stupid than worshiping a stone, an ox, an insect, more stupid than all that is—to worship under the name of God . . . a twaddler.

ATTACK UPON CHRISTENDOM
Søren Kierkegaard

CONTENTS

(xi)

Contents

(xii)

Preface

Ours is the first attempt in recorded history to build a culture upon the premise that God is dead. The period *post mortem Dei* divides into two distinct eras, roughly at some point between the World Wars. Until that time, the cultural death of God meant something *anti*-Christian; after it and until now, the death of God means something entirely *post*-Christian. The author of this book writes mainly about the latter, and this is his distinct contribution to the analysis of present-day culture. This preface undertakes to speak mainly of the former as *background* for an understanding of *post*-Christian culture and the death of God in the second sense.

To speak of "the death of God" in its anti-Christian meaning is to invoke at once the name of Friedrich Nietzsche, that great genius in pain finally made mad by his perception into the inner meaning of Western culture. With him, still, we have to ask about the death of God.

There are several stages in the myth Nietzsche tells of why and how God died. First, the many gods had to go. Theirs was not a doleful passing, although what followed was worse. The old deities did not "begloom" themselves to death. Rather, "a good joyful Deity-end had they!" They "*laughed* themselves to death once on a time!" This happened when "the ungodliest utterance came from a God himself"—when "an old grim-beard of a God, a jealous one, forgot himself in such a wise" as to say: "There is but one God! Thou shalt have no other Gods before me!" Then all the Gods "laughed, and shook upon their thrones." They exclaimed, "Is it not just divinity that there are Gods but no God?" and then they expired from god-shattering laughter such as only a god can enjoy.[1]

The God that remained, according to Nietzsche, had never as much life as they. He could neither laugh nor dance. Obeisance to Him was bound to be culture-destroying; His, the spirit of gravity. The old classical deities had at least the energy bestowed on them by the fact that each was closely identified with the nisus of some human need or with some force in nature. The one God was, after all, only a conjecture. Moreover, the rub was that, as a transcendent God, he was a conjecture that reached beyond man's creating will. This Nietzsche wished to estop, in order to liberate the cultural creativity of mankind. "I do not wish your conjecturing to reach beyond your creating will," he wrote.[2] After the gods made in man's image, the God who proposed to make and remake man in his own image, that God too had to die.

That is a more unsavory tale to tell. He was too much God-with-us, God in human, all-too-human form. He mixed too much in human affairs, even manifesting himself in this miserable flesh. In a sense, God's fellow-humanity killed him. Such a God must be wholly done to death, Nietzsche believed, else man as he now is would be certified from on high.

Man in his misery and weakness had a hand in this. Such was Nietzsche's vision of "the ugliest man," the epitome of all that should not receive divine endorsement but should be surpassed, "something sitting by the wayside shaped like a man, and hardly like a man, something nondescript." God's all-too-human pity and very un-Godlike demeanor was an offense to modesty. Therefore he had to be slain.

. . . he—*had to die*: he looked with eyes which beheld everything,—he beheld man's depths and dregs, all his hidden ignominy and ugliness.

His pity knew no modesty: he crept into my dirtiest corners. This most prying, over-intrusive, over-pitiful one had to die.

He ever beheld *me*: on such a witness I would have revenge—or not live myself.

The God who beheld everything, *and also man*: that God had to die! Man cannot *endure* that such a witness should live.[3]

Man could not endure the God who beheld him through and through. So man took "revenge on this witness,"[3] and became the murderer of the God who set and besets him in his existence, and does not turn away his eyes or refrain from knowing it altogether.

Nietzsche's portrayal of the one atheist who has complete certitude that God is dead was of "the last Pope," now "out of service." He "served that old God until his last hour." He was, so to speak, at the bedside when God breathed his last. Yet even he is not free from the gravity of pious recollections. This may be taken as a symbol of the modern "religiosity," Protestant and Catholic, analyzed so well by the author of the present volume—a religiosity unable quite to forget that God once lived, yet unable to face this modern world and live freely within its culture without attempting to impose extrinsic limits or so-called religious interpretations upon the cultural products of men.

God had to die in order that man might be what he is to become, in order that man may become the unlimited creator of culture. On the one hand, Nietzsche is willing to speak for modern man and say that "if there were a God [in the old sense of divinity], I could not endure not being He." On the other hand, he is the spokesman of modern man in saying that he cannot endure that divinity should exist in its Christian meaning, for man cannot live and work creatively if he endures that such a condescending witness of his existence should himself be alive. This was for Nietzsche the grandeur of man's freedom in exercise even in the midst of his ugliest misery, that he refuses to allow this God to face him, or face with him the task of creating those new worlds man alone wants to

(xvi)

shoulder. Man cannot be while God lives. He cannot be the self he would create, *or* the self he knows he actually is, while God remains significant in the world where autonomous man dwells. Such was Nietzsche's proposal as to what should be man's mode of being in this world, and his discerning description of man's actual mode of being in the modern period. To be alone in his cultural strength and future achievements, to be alone in his present weakness, and out of weakness to create his own strength by himself calling forth the things that are out of the things that are not—such is the enterprise of Western man in the present day. Therefore God had to die, and in his volume Professor Vahanian undertakes a cultural analysis of some of the laborious "religious" efforts to perform artificial respiration over the corpse. "Without God," Kierkegaard wrote with similar discernment into the present age, "man is [not too weak, but] too strong for himself."[4] Without God, man is at the same time not too strong but too weak for himself. Attempting to be half with, half without the living God, and without God to have his religiosity still, and being unable to endure the living God, man is too weak for the task he has assumed.

It is important for the reader to know what the author of this book means by the "living" God who until recently still shaped this culture from which he is more and more missing. It is necessary to understand his thesis that "God dies as soon as he becomes a cultural accessory of a human ideal," and that by virtue of "the radical immanentism of our cultural religiosity," no one can suppose there is any hope in immanent religion for the revival of God—no one, that is, who knows what was ever meant by the living God as the premise of all the cultural works of man. A modern man who still believed in God, Pascal, expressed thoughts pertinent to this problem. His statement of radical Christian monotheism simply repeats God's living relation to man which offended Nietzsche so deeply, and which modern religiosity also—in the author's definition of it—is far from believing under its many disguises:

> The Christian religion . . . teaches men these two truths; that there is a God whom men can know, and that there is a corruption in their nature which renders them unworthy of Him. It is equally important to men to know both these points; and it is equally dangerous for man to know God without knowing his own wretchedness, and to know his own wretchedness without knowing the Redeemer who can free him from it. The knowledge of only one of these points gives rise either to the pride of philosophers, who have known God, and not their own wretchedness, or to the despair of atheists, who know their own wretchedness, but not the Redeemer . . . We can have an excellent knowledge of God without that of our own wretchedness, and of our own wretchedness without that of God. But we cannot know Jesus Christ without knowing at the same time both God and our own wretchedness.[5]

This understanding of the living God shapes our understanding of the God who is now really absent. This denial men have made from at least the start of the modern period; and we are now beginning to act accordingly. We are beginning also to know in political and cultural terms what that denial means, as all along we might have known from the clairvoyance of many great minds who either urged or regretted the event of the living God's demise.

To speak of "the death of God" calls to mind the names of other great men. Dostoevski (whom Nietzsche referred to as "the only psychologist from whom I have learned anything") and the central figures in his novels: Roskolnikov, the door of the *acte gratuit* to see whether he could "step over barriers or not" in *Crime and Punishment*; Kirillov in *The Possessed* who expressed the fact that "the highest point of my self-will is to kill myself with my own hands . . . without any cause at all" but "to prove in the highest point my independenec and my new terrible freedom," and the revolutionaries in that same novel, and particularly their theoretician Shigalov, who starting from unlimited freedom came inexorably to unlimited despotism and boundless submission, and to "the last new principle of general destruction for the sake of the ultimate good"; and Ivan, in *The Brothers Karamazov*, who was the epitome of Euclidian reason in morality, which led logically in Ivan to the view that all things are permitted, and actually in his half-brother to the murder of their lecherous old father. Albert Camus, who documents the occurence of all that Dostoevski foresaw when in *The Rebel* he traces the steps from deicide to regicide to humanicide to conscientious murder or suicide and to boundless slavery and immorality without limits; and who declares forthrightly that "the philosophy of the age of enlightenment finally led to the Europe of the black-out."[6] One could mention also de Lubac's *The Drama of Atheistic Humanism*[7] which demonstrates what was so plain from the beginning in the case in Nietzsche, that atheism in the West is not simply non-theism but *anti*-theism and moreover that it is *anti*-Christ in its innermost meaning.

The contemporary age *post mortem Dei*, however, is not so much *anti*-Christian as *post*-Christian though still religious. "Where the world has not become an object of God's attack little remains but frosty discussion of God as Creator,"[8] and self-elected efforts to put ourselves in touch with him by means of conjectures thrown upon the blank screen of being that is said to be ultimate. This also means: where God has become a *datum* (sought, found, or missed) and not a living *mandatum,* little remains of vital significance for human affairs. Not that we do not have gods, and to spare. Like the *pre*-Christian Athenians, we *post*-Christians are a very religious people. Pale shadows of the pagan dieties—of sex and hearth, and battle, and of the city, civilization, and the outer spaces—have in fact returned to prevail over us. Such is the result of the, as yet, undissolved synthesis between divine and human creativity which the author of this book calls religiosity. "Men stand round in a circle and suppose," Robert Frost wrote, "while the secret sits in the middle and knows." Amid all this solemn

supposing, the author speaks for what W. K. Clif-
ford once called, "the still small voice that murmurs
'fiddlesticks.'"

While asking whether religiosity offers any hope
of reviving God in this post-Christian era, Mr.
Vahanian has a secondary theme close to his elbow
as he writes. This is the question whether without
the living God there can possibly be a fully human
culture. A most intriguing thing about this book is
the fact that the author seems to answer this question in the affirmative. To a large extent he goes
with this age in accepting the complete autonomy
of various spheres of culture. This culture is ana-
lytically described as resting on radical immanentism and not radical monotheism. It is no longer
anti-God. In the *anti*-Christian phase of "the death
of God," men were still determined culturally by
"pious recollections"—recollections of a dead God
who was still the mirror-image of the living Christ.
In the *post*-Christian phase of "the death of God,"
Western man is post-Christian *culturally* as well as
theologically. Atheism is not only a theoretical
claim made by exceptional rebels; it is now also a
practical possibility for countless men. The possibility of a practical and cultural atheism has been
achieved in this *post*-Christian age in the independence and immanentism of all spheres of culture—including, in the author's opinion, religion.
Find yourself and you will not need God; accomplish something in culture and evidently God is
superfluous.

"The last Pope out of service" yet still not free

from the gravity of pious recollections, is the proper symbol for the religiosity of the first phase of the death of God—a religiosity which secretly did not count on the living God yet was not quite able to let go of him altogether. What can serve, we may ask, as a fit symbol for the religiosity of the second and culturally *post*-Christian phase? Perhaps the picture Camus draws of two humanists, each "disclaiming divinity" as they prepare some historical action or cultural work: "They shall understand how they correct one another, and that a limit, under the sun, shall curb them all. *Each tells the other that he is not God.*"[9] Such was Camus' vision of a culture based on the intrinsic self-creativity and intrinsic self-moderation that would be forthcoming if all human life were made an *art*. While one humanist says this to another rather genially, half-humorously and without the dynamism of rebellion that affected the first modern men, there is here still too much memory of God for this fully to express the *post*-Christian period as Vahanian sees it. God is far more dead. The *present* religiosity simply does not understand the meaning of faith in the living God or of powerful rebellion.

And the *present* culture has achieved its autonomy and does not raise the question. It is based on the final achievement of the death of God now forgotten. *Post*-Christian culture is therefore a genuine possibility because it is an actuality. While the author may be mistaken in believing (if I do not misread him) that a culture based on the death of God can finally succeed in the attempt,

(xxii)

certainly his fine sensitivity for the cultural achievements of modern man enables him to see that many if not most or all revivals of religion in the present day seek to impose illegitimate limits on man's freedom to face the modern world and live freely within this culture.

I have chosen, however, in introducing the reader to this book, to prepare him for a most startling assertion in it: that since Christianity "universalized" and made relevant to the cultures of many nations the living God of the one people of Israel, the idea of "the death of God" is a purely Christian notion. "The irony of the cultural tradition of Christianity," Vahanian writes, is that "it has bequeathed us the idea of the death of God." The fact that "the missing God" is the missing Christ, or that modern atheistic humanism must be anti-Christian humanism, is evident everywhere in Sartre. This can be seen in the fundamental categories of his system of thought—indeed, in the very terms he uses—which apparently are designed to replace precisely the concept of the only living God, who is missing from modern Western culture. It is patent that since ('tis said) the living God of Israel was so much alive that he could become man and know him altogether, without any loss to his divine life, it has proved culturally impossible to "exclude God the Father" without a program for first excluding God the Son. Christ is the Word, and knowledge even, of that God who cannot longer be allowed in the land of the living.

This book, however, consists of straightforward

cultural analysis of the religious, political, artistic, literary, and societal movements of our era. This is an unhesitating, unflinching analysis of an age which, Vahanian believes, has no concern even to deny God. Every revival of Christianity in the past three hundred years has revived less of it, and each was less and less an enduring revival. Religion has become acculturated—adjusted to what was lost, to a world in which God is admitted only as a lack. The efforts of theologians and philosophers, as well as of other leaders in our intellectual and cultural life, to reshape this age from within its presuppositions, are examined and found wanting. For all these efforts, our culture remains—in Sartre's phrase—a lack lacking.

Moreover, there is an increasing population on the periphery or wholly outside the Western lineage: beat Zen, square Zen, and Zen Zen, and hotel lobby religions of all sorts but one. An awareness of this fringe segment of our culture implies no lack of human feeling for the spiritual plight of countless people, or insensitivity to the difficulty of opening windows toward an ultimate heaven in this urbanized and mechanistic society. One cannot but regard all this as a breakdown of tradition that is without parallel. As weapons technology and military hardware (based on the one distinctive accomplishment of modern Western man: his science) went precipitately "from the wheel to the whoosh,"[10] so Western religious faith has proceeded, and with this our culture itself, from the living God to a "whoosh." Modern man has not the

(xxiv)

power in himself to be a Captain Ahab—if, indeed, Ahab was. It is more and more impossible for us even to curse God and to mean what we say because we have lost the meaning of the cipher God —the living God—who may have us in his clutches. Were we at all like Ahab, we might have some ground for supposing that a new age of faith may yet dawn.

Professor Vahanian finds no evidence for such a conclusion from his analysis of the ingredients of an immanently religious culture. The evidence points only to a God who once lived and whose reality cannot be recovered from within this post-Christian culture. For God to be meaningfully dead he had to have been once meaningfully alive. The author of this book is apt to disagree with this, but it seems to me that it is still the case that the premise of contemporary culture (except in the sphere of autonomous science) is not merely the absence of theistic presuppositions, but the real absence of a God who formerly lived and had his dealings with men. It means "the death of God" still present. Probing still more deeply, the author questions whether such a God was livingly present to the so-called Christendom of medieval culture. This, if true, would mean that he was long a-dying —not so much by the rebellion and revulsion that have characterized the resolute atheists of the modern period, as by each stage of apparently triumphant interpenetration of a so-called Christian culture making him an appendage of man's cultural work and institutions. In any case, by "the death of

God" the author has in mind a decisive turning away from the notion of the biblical Deity.

The author's analysis may seem to reach strictly negative conclusions. This will surprise many readers who note that he is a professor of religion and that his is the Protestant persuasion. But the apparent negativity of the conclusions drawn from this cultural analysis has itself to be strictly understood. A discerning reader need not have it pointed out that the author's own convictions may not be those of the period he examines, much less that he believes that God can in reality be slain, for all the magnificent modern Western attempt to do this. He simply refuses to credit the excessively endorsed protests that Lo, here and Lo, there He is alive, when the religious fingers point to much worship and devotion going on. The worship goes on, it is true, but to deities that are the product of the fertile mind of man—which Calvin called a perfect factory of idolatry—and who have only such life as their identity with man's cultural vitality bestows on them.

Not improperly, therefore, I may draw upon two astounding footnotes which Sartre drops in the course of his ontological analysis of man's mode of being in a world in which God is dead, to indicate Vahanian's mind on the subject of the age he unpacks in the course of this volume. One may doubt whether Sartre has any basis for saying any such thing. Still it is remarkable that he wrote, toward the end of his own relentless analysis: "These considerations do not exclude the possibility of an ethics of deliverance and salvation. But this can be achieved only after a radical conversion which we cannot discuss here"; and earlier: ". . . this supposes a self-recovery of being . . . [which] we shall call authenticity, the description of which has no place here."[11] One cannot imagine what sort of radical transformation of man's existence from the one he describes, Sartre may have had in mind. In any case, the promise remains unfulfilled.

The broad outlines of Vahanian's more positive analysis of a possible very human and very theocentric culture are clear, even if quite properly he refrains from discussing this here. He would certainly hold that gods that are conjectures reaching only a bit beyond man's cultural enterprises and drawing their life from this, are not transcendent enough to be living gods; and at the same time that every attempt of any age to be religious in this way bestows just enough life upon such deities for them in turn to prove inhumanly oppressive and to suck up into themselves the wellsprings of cultural creativity from which they spring by an immanent act of God-creation. In contrast, the transcendent God who lives his own life and creates man in his own image already has deity enough and is in no need of extrinsically limiting man's cultural life. From afar he can be unobtrusively near in the midst of man's work in culture. Only a living God can let man live, allowing him room to express himself and preserving him and all his accomplishments as wholly other than himself. The question is not whether God exists, but whether *man is*, and is a free creator of culture.

It was the living God, wholly unconstrained and

unhurried in his eternity, who said, Let there be light, saw then that this was so, and judged it to be a splendid thing in its own right. Only a living God can say: Let man be. Idols exact a greater tribute whenever man lets them be. Only a God who from afar faces human culture leaves room for human action freely facing toward him and toward unfettered cultural enterprises. This ground for the self-recovery of modern man (precisely not a *self*-recovery but still a recovery of self in the midst of his cultural history), the description of which has no place here, must wait for the book Professor Vahanian has in him to write on "Protestantism and the Arts" or "Protestantism and Culture." If he does this, he will walk the narrow ridge between every form of religious heteronomy prejudicial to culture on the one hand and, on the other, an assertive humanistic autonomy on which (it is about time we drew the proper conclusion from the now long drawn-out attempt) it is not possible to build a culture worthy of the name, but only an inhumane civilization.

Professor Vahanian obviously prefers the independent cultural creations of an age from which even the memory of God has disappeared, to an age in which everything has to be stained with a little religiosity. He wants no going back to a "Christian culture" even if that were possible. Contemporary men should banish nostalgia and freely engage in the cultural enterprises of this present age premised as it is on the death of God. It is not impossible that fundamentally the freedom to go with this culture in its independence may be the only way to go with a God who is at all a living God. For the "living" God means the "freedom" of God. The radical freedom of God in his own transcendent life apart from man means that man has room to breathe. It also means that God is free to be inexpressibly near without driving human freedom out of the world or derogating upon the form or the substance of man's cultural creativity. It may be that by freely engaging in the production of a humanistic culture, a new approach (to speak improperly) will be found to the free and living God. Or to speak more properly: only in the course of free and originating cultural action is He to be expected, and not by the revival of some dead cultural god of the past. Amid a *de*-divinized historical epoch God may be found to be alive. At least, this is more to be expected than that God can become alive in a *re*-divinized culture.

PAUL RAMSEY

Princeton University
Christmas, 1960.

Foreword

FOR BETTER or for worse, the dominant religious patterns of Western culture have been inspired and shaped by Christianity. Christianity has been the religion of the West; and Western culture, with its achievements and its failures, would be unthinkable apart from the spirit of Christianity and the Christian understanding of man and of the world, of reality and of God.

Sympathizers and detractors of religion alike can agree that the essence of Christianity is embodied in the cultural realizations of the West. They must, however, ask the question whether or not these achievements, not to mention the failures, have resulted today in the self-invalidation of Christianity. Circumstances seem to indicate that they have. In the present situation Western culture may even be said to demand its emancipation from Christianity. Even the Christian must concede that the situation requires either an almost inconceivable reconstruction of Christianity or the emancipation of Western culture from Christianity in its present condition. Just as in the name of liberty, of the dignity of man, and of self-determination, the former colonies are now repudiating the nations which (though sometimes unwittingly) taught them the meaning of these ideals, Western culture is weaning itself from that Christian spirit which has so far nurtured it.

The legacy of Christianity includes not only moribund religious phenomena and vestigial—if apparently strong—ecclesiastical institutions, as well as unique museums of the creative imagination and the artistic mind; it also includes science and scientism, technology and the addiction to material and spiritual gadgets. Our culture is no longer transcendentalist but immanentist; no longer sacral or sacramental, but secularistic or profane. This transition is explained by the fact that the essentially mythological world-view of Christianity has been succeeded by a thoroughgoing scientific view of reality, in terms of which either God is no longer necessary, or he is neither necessary nor unnecessary: he is irrelevant—he is dead. The question of existence no longer leads, as was often presumed in the past, to the question of God either necessarily or logically.

In this light, in the following pages I attempt to show historically but briefly some antecedents of this gradual corrosion and self-invalidation of Christianity. Presenting, then, the case for a new Christian culture which is made by certain contemporary Christian thinkers, I try to show how and why our civilization contradicts this case, its imperviousness to Christianity, its cultural incapacity for, as well as disavowal of, God. From this point of view the so-called religious revival of the preceding decade marks the transition from the Christian to the post-Christian era; simultaneously Christian (let alone atheistic) existentialism, unlike many previous Christian theologies or philosophies, makes it impossible to identify God with man—perhaps because God is dead.

The fundamentals of modern culture are neither non-Christian nor anti-Christian; they are post-Christian. They are derived from Christianity, yet in them Christianity suffers "not a torture death but a quiet euthanasia." It may be that our age still is religious. But it is certainly post-Christian.

GABRIEL VAHANIAN

Syracuse, New York
December, 1960

PART ONE

THE RELIGIOUS AGONY OF CHRISTIANITY

CHAPTER I

Modern Religiosity and the Christian Tradition

THE essence of Christianity, in the highest hours of man's faith in God, manifested itself (in C. S. Lewis's words) in drawing man away from gossiping about God. The strange fate of Christianity in its modern dress is precisely that it has reduced man to the futility of idly gossiping about God. Our interest in religion goes no deeper and is no less irresponsible than Adam's curiosity about the knowledge of good and evil. But what, from a theological point of view, curiosity and gossip alike indicate is the same pseudo concern that is characteristic of religiosity. Religiosity is to the communion of saints, which is cemented together by the bonds of a common faith in God, as the Peeping Tom is to society or to the family. Morbid curiosity is no less morbid for expressing a certain concern, if this concern is in itself basically inauthentic. The Peeping Tom is not a lover because he will not assume the responsibility of such

a role. Religiosity is not faith. In religious curiosity, man substitutes superstition for faith in God.
And superstition is a crude attempt to build a coherent universe which will compensate for an inner incoherence. Failing to resolve the contradictions of life, superstition seeks to justify these
contradictions; in an admittedly awkward way, it
seeks for a principle of consistency. Religiosity,
though it may be a slight improvement on superstition, only serves to fill the vacuum created by
the breakdown of man's understanding of himself
and his relation to the universe and to the human
community. In the last analysis, religiosity is an
expression of sublimated loneliness, and for this
reason is often collectivistic in its manifestations.
It is also the symptom of a suppressed doubt, of
a subliminal faithlessness resulting from failure to
admit that faith in God offers doubt as its corollary.

Accordingly, it would be erroneous to interpret
the collectivism which underlies today's manifestations of religiosity to mean that modern man has
finally recognized the need for a rediscovery of the
communal dimension of existence. Nothing could
be further from the truth. The fact is that collectivism is but another face of the many aspects an
unreconstructed individualism can present. The
respective extravagances of collectivism and individualism are equally irresponsible and equally
irrational; they are equally without justification
from a Christian point of view.

To the extent that modern religiosity is partly

(4)

a Protestant extravagance, Protestantism has been unable to foster, other than sporadically and on a limited scale, anything comparable to the Catholic consciousness of a common bond (even though this bond has been dualistically understood, i.e. in terms of the orders of nature and of grace). More often than not, Protestants have understood the New Testament demand for radical obedience as a demand for radical individualism, oblivious to the fact that obedience also entails common allegiance. It is no wonder, then, that the recent revival of religion has been neither radical nor an act of obedience. It has no other allegiance than to its own inauthenticity. And it is inauthentic because it reduces religion to a feeling of togetherness, which is to community as the romantic subjectivistic feeling of absolute dependence is to the Biblical concept of creatureliness, or as faith in faith is to true faith. Togetherness is a substitute sense of community, a counterfeit communion. This amounts to saying that the recent revival promotes the feeling that one can be religious and can even have faith in God by proxy. It is evident that no one can live another man's faith, just as no one can die another man's death. The question then rises from our memory of Western history and its immediate religious and philosophical back ground: Is not religiosity by proxy man's overt attempt to evade the reality that he has killed God, and does it not indicate that he will not face this fact, let alone assume responsibility for the deed?

To be sure, the recent upsurge of religiosity at

least reminds us that it is an unavoidable constituent of human existence (albeit a negative one), and that it will always remain so. But this can be stated only in the same sense as one says that death is ineluctably a part of life. Just as death is loss of being, so religiosity is loss of faith in God. Death constantly threatens existence, as religiosity threatens faith in God.

The modern period in general and the contemporary upsurge of interest in religion in particular have made clear something which has never been properly acknowledged in either Christian or non-Christian circles. This is the existential fact that, both theoretically and practically, God's death is not accidental. It belongs wholly to, and is grounded in, man's natural inclination to religiosity. The death of God, therefore, cannot be viewed in any way as a recent historical or cultural misfortune which a revival, be it of religiosity or even of authentic faith, will overcome. The death of God is not an accident, an accessory, or nonessential, accompaniment of existence; it is not a diversion, but a fundamental possibility which confronts every man. Briefly and simply, it corresponds to the serpent's *eritis sicut dii* in the Biblical myth of Adam's fall. And just as Adam was responsible for his own fall, so is this post-Christian era the product of Christianity.

Consequently, the Christian faith today is neither coextensive nor even partly contiguous with man's faithlessness. According to the Christian tradition it has always been implicit, if not

(6)

Vah. more conserv.
than A + H in claiming man
is relig. by nature.

explicit, that faith in God (as well as God's faithfulness to man) is somehow bound up with man's
faithlessness: "Lord, I believe; help Thou mine unbelief." No longer, it appears, is this so. It seems
that the Christian faith has ceased to provide for
unbelief. As a result, the Christian concept of man
has been devalued. It offers no point of contact to
modern man, because his self-understanding is
completely divergent from the Christian concept.
Emphatically, it is not simply a question of the
loss of the sacramental dimension manifest in the
classical Christian image of man. Nor is it a question of the loss of the sacral dimension so in-
delibly characteristic of past stages of Western
culture. The loss is incomparably greater and
deeper. It has affected man's outlook on life, his
raison d'être, and his view of reality. To use a
scholastic distinction, what has taken place is not
a mere transformation, but a transubstantiation.
The transition (for want of a better term) is more
like that of China before and after the Communist
accession to power than like that of Europe before
and after the Reformation.

The Reformation changed the form but not the
content of Christianity. It affected dogmas and
rituals, but not the faith that these were intended
to proclaim. It altered the structure of the Church
but not its reality, its foundation. The change today
resides in the very content of the Christian faith
itself. What is unacceptable is not the religio-cultural tradition of Christianity, but the very source
of this tradition. More precisely, today's protest is

directed against the core itself of the Christian faith in that the latter is felt to be not only exhausted but also incompatible with, contemptuous of, and inimical to the actual situation of man. The essence of Christianity is felt as alien to man's condition, and, of course, it must be admitted that organized Christianity has often degraded and enslaved man, and deprecated his creative imagination and the intrinsic worth of his finitude.

Indeed, it is historically verifiable that Christianity when it is organized is less apt than when it is not organized to inform and transform genuinely and creatively its secular cultural background. The evidence of the sects as well as of early Christianity helps to corroborate this assertion. When Christianity became organized, it almost immediately arrogated to itself what rightly belonged to culture and to the sphere of the secular. Medieval Christianity may legitimately be cited as an illustration of this tendency toward usurpation. It is not that the spiritual concern of Christianity should be insulated and preserved from pervading the secular goals and aspirations of man. (Indeed, this has often been the religious and cultural heresy of the sects.) But the spiritual can only usurp the prerogatives of and negate the secular by assimilation into the structures of organized religion. For there is nothing about these structures which is intrinsically spiritual. Structures are either cultural or neutral, even when they support the essence of Christianity. When organized religion thus associates itself with secular

(8)

structures and, unnecessarily, fuses with them, it
deprives both the spiritual (or faith) and culture
of their reciprocal freedom. It may be more accurate to say that as a result of this fusion Christianity is forced on the world and on culture. But even
more important, under such circumstances the
spiritual loses its intrinsic worth and becomes but
one among rival cultural influences. Organized
Christianity transforms the gospel into a tradition
to be accepted without the exercise of individual
decision, even as it transforms faith into a cultural
pattern which, naturally enough, seeks its own
preservation and perpetuation.

If it is true that the sects, better than organized
churchly Christianity, exemplify the reality of
spiritual communion stemming from an individual's decision in faith, then it may be asserted that
churchly Christianity does not transform the world,
but enslaves it. Enslavement, however, works both
ways and not one way alone. It implies the petrifaction of Christianity, which is another mode of
Christianity's loss of relevance. Enslavement, or
spiritual colonialism, comes to be substituted for
the spiritual world-facing and world-honoring responsibility that springs from the vocation of faith
itself. Seen in this light the age of colonialism now
fretfully drawing to a close with the aura of a
mal du siècle can be interpreted as the political
and cultural replica, if not direct application, of
a tradition-bound and spiritually colonialist organized Christianity. Would it not be rational to say
that the decadence of imperialism, with which in-

(9)

dubitably Christianity was entangled, spells the decadence of religious patterns and structures as we have known them? It is possible that the fate of Christianity still depends on an unsuspected demonstration of its power of self-apprehension. Unfortunately, Christianity is too intimately, even inextricably, bound up with patterns and structures which, having become secularized, are likely to prevent such a demonstration.

An organized Christianity does not simulate the patterns of the spirit. Nor is there any inconsistency in referring to patterns of the spirit. They can be distinguished from those of the world, and this distinction is not qualitative only; it is also quantitative. To contrast the two, one can say that the patterns of the spirit are prophetic, while those of the world and those of an organization are institutional or tradition-bound. The prophetic spirit does not deny the world and its traditions or its organizations. It even makes use of them. But it does not wed itself to them. Nor does it enslave them. Were it to do so, the prophetic spirit would lose its own identity, its own authenticity.

It is highly significant that the renowned Church historian, Kenneth S. Latourette, should regard the nineteenth century as the great century of Christianity, because the latter's global expansion was possible largely on account of its intricate organization; and that Sören Kierkegaard, who lived in the nineteenth century, not unlike a prophet, excoriated Christianity for having submitted to the inauthentic mores imbedded in and fettered by its cultural accommodations and compromises. Now, as then, today and always, the Christian problem is to correlate the truth of Christianity with the empirical truths men live by, without confusing them: man cannot live by one or the other kind of truth alone.

Paul Tillich, in his *Systematic Theology*,[1] writes that "theology moves back and forth between two poles, the eternal truth of its foundations and the temporal situation in which the eternal truth must be received." In as much as theology represents that form of knowledge which "in all its forms and degrees besides being an understanding of its object is simultaneously an existential understanding of one's self in 'faith,' "[2] Tillich's definition of theology can be applied to Christianity itself. The temporal situation of the nineteenth century was definitely imbued with an optimistic view of man and a general progressivism. To say, as some theologians do, that the nineteenth-century religious thinkers at once neglected both the poles mentioned by Tillich is to blind oneself to the fact that these thinkers did after all speak to their situation. This should not be minimized, even if their efforts later proved to be disastrous, since without doubt not only did the nineteenth-century thinkers speak to the situation of that time, but they also went so far as to adapt the spiritual foundation of Christianity to the structures of that situation. That is why the evidences of spiritual earnest and missionary zeal were by far grievously counterbalanced by the anonymous victory of the secular

NB.

here's why Barth's revolt never fully took hold in U.S. — we were too much in Social gospel.

(11)

structures and their goals, to which Christianity in effect bowed down. In doing so, Christianity was killing Western culture, just as Western culture was killing Christianity.[3]

But, if the decay of Christianity is partially due to its culturally superannuated structures, it also has its source in the sclerosis and the expropriation of the Christian faith itself. As was pointed out earlier, faith is no longer contingent upon unfaith. The contingency has ceased either because religious faith is dead or because unfaith, once satisfied, cannot help but be self-reliant; or for both these reasons. But there is a still more important reason: it is the severance of doubt from faith: "Lord, I believe; help Thou mine unbelief." Only the unbeliever can believe: only the sinner can be justified. He who believes, believes as only an unbeliever can. He who is justified, is justified as only a sinner can be. Whatever else modern man is, he is not an unbeliever and not a sinner in the Biblical sense. Why? Because faith, in the Biblical sense, is dead. It is not essential to man's unfaith. It has estranged itself from doubt. And it is human to doubt. As Unamuno observed, while Christianity lay dying before him, "a faith which does not doubt is a dead faith."[4]

Looking at the contemporary situation of religiosity, with the sense of agony with which Unamuno penetrated the meaning of Christianity, one may wholly agree with him that, today, faith entertains no doubt. It is much too monolithic and doctrinaire—much too hopeless. Indeed, only through hope can faith doubt. For hope is an integral element of faith. But so is doubt—even to the extent that the element of hope can doubt and the element of doubt can hope.

In the present age doubt has become immune to faith and faith has dissociated itself from doubt. Nothing is worse than a dead faith, except a dead doubt.

When doubting no longer liberates the moment of faith or propels the movement of faith, it is quite likely that faith has become petrified and threatened with self-extinction, and that this condition threatens with extinction the cultural forms to which such rigid faith was wedded. Remarking how the scorpion injects its poison into its own head when it is caught in a fatal situation like a fire, Unamuno then raises the question whether Christianity and our civilization are not committing a similar suicide. Is not indeed the literature of "peace of mind," of "mental health," a poison which is now attacking the head of Christianity—the heart presumably having stopped long since?

CHAPTER II

The Dishabilitation of the Christian Tradition

SINCE the advent of the modern period the Biblical view of man and the world has so deteriorated that it has no means of commanding the response and assent of the modern mind. For the sake of convenience, the gradual elimination of the Biblical view can be best observed in the cultural climate created by Protestantism. And it is still more tangible in the development of American Protestantism.

Two points must be clarified right away. First, neither Protestantism as a movement nor Protestantism in America is solely responsible for this elimination: it is just that the transition from the Christian to the post-Christian era is most clearly exemplified in the Protestant tradition. Second, a brief definition of the now allegedly eliminated Biblical view is necessary. Succinctly stated, this view is transcendentalist. Man and the world are God's creation; therefore God is

(14)

wholly other than what he creates and neither man
nor the world is conceived as a self-sufficient and
self-reliant entity. Owing to the elimination of
this view, an immanentist understanding of man's
nature and of the world's reality has successfully come into its own. The modern view thus
stands in direct opposition to the Biblical conception. Between them a leveling down has taken
place.

The three features of this leveling down are all
present in American Protestantism, and this is why
it represents so aptly the radical dishabilitation of
the Christian tradition as a whole.

The first feature deals with the translation, in
the American imaginary vision, of the Christian
concept of the new man into the secular concept
of the New Adam and, subsequently, into that of
the Christ-figure. The progression thus begins with
the Biblical understanding of the new man in
Christ, who himself is the second, the New Adam,
and moves through the concept of man himself as
the new Adamic man to the final concept of
Christic man.

The second feature concerns the idea of the
Kingdom of God. Relevant precisely because it
is utopian—since it has no appointed time or
place, is present yet always coming—it becomes
turgescent and irrelevant as soon as, transmigrat-
ing into Millenarianism and the American Dream,
it is domesticated by and conformed to the
immanentism of religiosity.

The third feature is characteristic of the Social

Gospel movement. No doubt recapitulating in part certain compelling themes of the second feature, especially those relating to the presence of the Kingdom, the Social Gospel originally laid undivided stress on the urgency of their actuality. It did not reject the soteriological elements of traditional Christianity (*i.e.* those dealing with individual salvation); yet it understood these in terms of their application to social problems, and aimed at combatting and extirpating evil and injustice. Emerging into prominence in the latter decades of the nineteenth century, the Social Gospel was the impassioned advocate of a much-needed *applied Christianity*. Represented by such men as Washington Gladden, the movement reached its incomparable height of expression in the person of Walter Rauschenbusch, whose work is a clear landmark of the Christian era. And yet, especially in the thought of Epigoni such as Josiah Strong, one can unmistakably detect deleterious traces of (in Richard Niebuhr's phrase) the "acculturation of Christianity." In this connection, it is not superfluous to add that a similarly deleterious acculturation can be felt *mutatis mutandis* in Roman Catholic documents of the same period, such as the papal encyclical *Rerum Novarum*. It is this acculturation that will preoccupy us here.

Let us consider how the concept of the Biblical new man in Christ is changed for that of secular Adamic man and, finally, for that of Christic man, the whole process spelling out the secularization of the Christ-event (*i.e. God's* redemptive act through the person and the work of Jesus Christ).

Man: From the New Adam of Faith to the Christic Man of Religiosity

Protestantism for the most part discarded all tradition; but except for the first phase of Protestantism in America, this repudiation cannot be described as a liberating movement toward "the original and eternal life out of which all tradition takes its rise."[1] That this repudiation was intended to unfetter the heart of the original Christian gospel and let it live anew, no one can deny. No one can overlook, however, the fact that such an attitude actually countenanced the emergence of secularism and indirectly encouraged its progress. It is significant that unexpected light is thrown on this matter by the development of American literature itself. In its magnificent self-appraisal we find, indeed, peculiar corroboration of the gradual de-Christianization of Western culture. Not that by inclination or design the American novelist was more iconoclastic and secularly minded than any other. But within his framework, he had only a culture without tradition. From this source his inspiration sprang, and in it the human scene of his imaginary vision was laid. That civilization was without cultural tradition, just as Protestantism was without religious tradition. Furthermore, in this case, the lack of cultural tradition actually derived from a lack of religious tradition. What brought about this lack of tradition, and what impact does it have?

American religion, on the whole faithful to the

theology of the Reformation, which was offered
as a return to Christian sources, seems appropriately to have considered itself as a new beginning.
It was as if the whole heritage of Christendom,
and especially of medieval Christianity, became
suddenly rejected or unacknowledged when the
first settlers arrived to these shores. Indeed, the
Pilgrim had a number of characteristics in common with Biblical man. Like the latter, either he
was a nomad or his rootage in the American soil
was so recent that he could identify himself with
those newly converted pagans, the early Christians, in being rooted in the soil of a new religion.
One can say without exaggeration that the Pilgrim
presented in many respects all the behavioral patterns of the new man, reborn in Christ, the new
Adam. But he was not simply the first Adam, nor
was his own beginning simply a recrudescence of
the primeval genesis of man; he was much more:
in Christ he was himself *a new* Adam, naming the
things and beings of the *new* Jerusalem. In all this,
stress must be laid on the epithet *new*. It is all-
important to note this point: the American Pilgrim
not only began anew; not only did he begin where
the first creature, Adam, did; but he began where
the new Adam begins—in the Kingdom of God.

It is in this sense that one can fathom the significance of the Puritans' repudiation of tradition.
And in this sense there is no doubt that such a step
meant for them a return to the original source. It
also meant a rejection of all intermediate interpretations of that source, whether theological or

cultural. Not only was the Pilgrim a new Adam, his surrounding itself was new—like a new Eden, or a new covenant, a new Jerusalem, a new Kingdom. The repudiation of tradition was thus effected for the sake of a stronger religious fidelity, in the name of a greater and more authentic allegiance to God. But this allegiance and this fidelity were soon to be severed from any sound or vitally religious reason for the repudiation of tradition. The outcome was the myth of an absolutely new beginning, not in God but in one's self, the myth of Adamic man.[2] This new doctrine best expressed itself in the nineteenth century. By that time the secularization of the new Adam had been completed, though the end had not yet been reached.

It is not unimportant to note that the creation of this myth about Adamic man was associated with an insistence on the part of literary men and critics that America should at last separate itself from Europe and attend to her own sources of inspiration and expression. By 1850 Realism in American art was developing independently of its European model. Religiously, America had already separated from Europe, though from a different motive. In literature and art the reasons for the separation were purely secular; certainly they were not informed by religious considerations. Could this have been the case if the religious voice had not already ceased to make itself heard? It seems that traditional Christianity had indeed been silenced, even if Hawthorne still was able to "understand" Puritan culture, though he did not agree with it. But by any interpretation, the trend revealed by Emerson or Whitman is definitely toward investing with pseudo-religious import the mythical attributes of the new secularized Adam. Meanwhile, hope and faith were replaced by progress and the natural goodness of man, a man ultimately bound neither to God nor to nature.

It is this Adam who in the novel of the twentieth century is to become the Christ-figure. And thus Adamic man is finally succeeded by Christic man. But in either case man usurps the role of Christ, by arrogating to himself Christ's very attributes. The Christ-figure of many contemporary novels does not indicate a return to the original source after pulling down the barriers of traditionalism. Rather, in a poignant way due to the tragedies of the age, it points to the uselessness of both tradition and the original source. And the tendency to universalize the qualities of Christ suggests but another aspect of the leveling-down and general immanentism by which this century of Western culture is best characterized.[3]

The Kingdom of God: Relevant as Utopia, Irrelevant as Religiosity

The idea of the Kingdom of God, in American Protestantism and its satellite religiosities, represents the antinomy between the classical Christian conception of a God-bound history and the present immanentist if ideological understanding of it. The preceding section showed that the self-made image of Adamic man actually perverted the Biblical conception of the new Adam. This section will show how Millenarianism was the great corrupter of the original Puritan conception of God's Kingdom.

The Protestant understanding of the Kingdom had always succeeded in preventing its identification with secular achievements, regardless of their eminence. For that reason, the Kingdom was always conceived of as an eschatological reality; that is to say, it was present here and now, but the here and now never became equated with eternity itself. As divine activity, the Kingdom was thought to inform and guide human activity; but never were these two activities identified. Rather, God's sovereignty (which is another way of speaking about God's Kingdom) always stood in judgment over man's undertakings and successes. No matter how faithfully a man trusted in God, his achievements were not to be considered as God's progressive revelation. Yet they were symbols of God's presence—of his *real* presence. They were symbols of God's sovereignty. They meant that God is the ruler of the universe, including this patch of land put under man's transitory but irrefragable responsibility.

It is this understanding of the Kingdom of God which H. Richard Niebuhr calls the dominant idea of early American Christianity. In his book *The Kingdom of God in America,* he shows how the original meaning of God's sovereignty, later understood as the "reign of Christ," was finally replaced by the notion of a divine kingdom on earth. This notion, though it gave birth to ethical theories and goals which were timely, none the less was unfortunately weaned on the evolutionary optimism of a declining theological liberalism. Two things are to be noted here.

First, Millenarianism appears to be the factor which corrupted the idea of the Kingdom of God into that of an earthly kingdom. The significance of the transition can be seen in the fact that the initial notion of God's sovereignty never resulted in any kind of tradition-bound and hierarchical, or hierocratic, structure; whereas the utopia of an earthly kingdom could not be indulged in without codifying the modes of God's sovereign presence, reducing them to and finally identifying them with the structures of finite realities. "So far as the Kingdom of Christ is set up in the world," wrote Jonathan Edwards, "so far is the world brought to an end, and the eternal state of things set up—so far are all the great changes and revolutions in the world brought to their everlasting issue, and all things come to their ultimate period."[4]

In this theology the Kingdom of Christ is envisioned as gradually taking over the changes wrought by the revolutions of this world. It evolves out of them as well as through them. When evolution replaced the idea of history sustained by, though not identical with, a divine purpose, the goal remained the same as before even though it no longer symbolized the same event, namely, the advent of Christ's reign on earth. Millenarianism thus institutionalized God's sovereignty. As such, it was an element of petrifaction, serving to devitalize Christianity. It blunted the incisiveness of God's sovereign presence. In fact, whether God was present or not and whether he was sovereign or not made no difference under an immanental optimism. It is strange as well as ironic that a society where authority, both political and religious, is defined in terms of God's immediate and direct dominion should result in one where God's rulership is purely nominal or at best constitutional. The perfectionistic yet conventional ideal of the millennium evolved out of a perverted notion of God's kingdom was promoted by this notion's concomitant loss of relevance. Translated into purely secular terms, it led to the hope that better societies will be born when better cars are built and more gadgets (material and spiritual alike) inundate our lives.

Second, the insistence on God's immediate dominion properly explains the absence of tradition within Protestantism, because it brings the present into focus and stresses that no social or political or even religious theory is to be identified with God's governance. A new tradition comes into being with the advent of every new generation. In the religious realm, this points to the urgent task which a church that must continually reform itself is called to perform. In the political realm, it establishes the principle and requires the practice of criticism, particularly self-criticism. Simultaneously, it places the political community itself under divine guidance and judgment.

To be sure, the absence of tradition never was quite absolute. But it was a seminal principle. That is to say, as a principle, it did not have to rely on institutions in order to be transmitted from one generation to the next. What was transmitted was not an objective tradition confined to rituals and institutions, but the principle which the traditional rituals and institutions symbolized. It is for this reason that when the principle declined in its vigor, the institutions alone could not revive it. When it died, the institutions managed to survive it, but they no longer symbolized God's sovereignty here and now. Simultaneously, they became secularized. "Henceforth the Kingdom of the Lord [is] a human possession, not a permanent revolution."[5]

Richard Niebuhr further believes that the institutionalization of God's dominion led to nationalism. Indeed, America once arrogated to itself the title of chosen nation, oblivious—as Israel once was—to the admonition of the prophets that it is God who chooses his people and not vice versa. Chosenness is not based on man's initiative: it is God's prerogative. Otherwise, God becomes a possession of the nation; to it, he becomes subordinate. Indeed, as the evidence shows, Christianity in this country is equated with democracy and culture, with progress and the American dream,[6] while on the Continent it is identified with the superiority of European culture and its surreptitious imperialism. In this respect, it is highly sig-

nificant that the institutions of the medieval Holy
Roman Empire were to a large extent founded on
a sacramentarianism which supported the hierarchy of separate yet co-ordinated articulations of
church and society. The sacramentarian dichotomy
between spiritual and secular was the compromise
that the imperialism of an institutionalized Christianity could and did then reach. The effect of
Millenarianism was that Protestantism institutionalized itself and, instead of the dualistic and otherworldly sacramentarianism of the Middle Ages,
it fostered a monistic and this-worldly "sacramentarianism" summed up by the secularized ideal of
a divine kingdom on earth.

Drained and etiolated, this ideal shows to what
extent the original trust in God's immediate sovereignty had deteriorated. Originally that sovereignty was experienced as a present reality underlying all human beings and their social as well as
religious aspirations and obligations. In the second
stage, God's sovereignty was, so to speak, sublimated, intellectualized, or even supernatural-
ized: the Kingdom of heaven was so construed
that Christ himself took on the appearances of a
judge who shall sift the elect from the reprobate.
It needs to be said that this kind of dualism, which
separates Christians from non-Christians, inevit-
ably amounts to a fundamental admission that
faith is losing its relevance to the present. The con-
versionist zeal which accompanies such radical
otherworldliness is evidence enough that the transcendental hope which once was incarnate in

(2 5)

earthly tasks and responsibilities (as it ought to be) has now evaporated into speculative visions of ethereal if celestial structures. When the third stage arrives, the immediacy of God's sovereignty here and now has already become a myth. At least, it is no longer effectual. While the autonomy of the earlier communities and the freedom of man were predicated on the idea of God's direct governance, the dualistic remoteness of God's heaven now no longer guarantees any present purpose to man's destiny and to the communal dimension of his existence.

When the Puritans settled on these shores they believed, as Edward Johnson wrote, that Jesus Christ intended "to manifest his kingly office toward his churches more fully than ever yet the sons of men saw." And though they believed also that—again in Johnson's words—"this is the place where the Lord will create a new heaven and a new earth in, new churches and a new commonwealth together,"[7] they did not imagine that an earthly city could ever be coextensive with the City of God. The Puritans did not think the City of God a spatial reality so much as a figure of speech denoting God's transcendental yet immediate governance of all things. The City of God meant for them that no earthly city could be self-sufficient, since the rule of God, which actually provided the principle of criticism and self-criticism, always stood in judgment over men's judgments and decisions. It meant that no finite achievement was final, but was always in need of God's grace. Such, too, was the inner meaning of the question they

(2 6)

were intimately habituated to ponder: "What is the chief end of man?" And their reply was: "Man's chief end is to glorify God, and enjoy Him forever."

Not inappropriately, Samuel Willard could then write that "the object of man's happiness is out of himself. Man cannot be his own felicity. He is a dependent creature; his being and his blessedness are two things. He cannot dwell at home. He doth not enjoy in himself a self-sufficiency."[8] The Puritans were strangers on this earth. That means, for them the earth was not eternal, nor self-sufficient, but transitory. Their understanding of existence was neither geocentric nor anthropocentric. And although heaven sounds as if it were their real home, it was nothing other than the principle on which they built their temporary dwellings, their communities, and their churches. In spatial terms, it meant that man is a dependent *creature*, answerable to the Lord who created everything, and particularly for all that over which man exerts his domination. No less than this constituted the phenomenological reality on which the Puritans based their understanding of existence and human destiny.[9]

If this seems outlandish, it is because the intervening Millenarian spirit has now become wholly secularized. It has completely adulterated the Pilgrim's empirical faith in God's immediate sovereignty.

The millennium is to one form of Christianity as the classless society is to communistic Marxism—a Moloch, which the present must appease with all its energies, both human and material or cultural. But once the millennium showed its real face—namely, that it was the fantastic construction of a speculative though religious ideology—man then discarded it and began to pretend that he enjoyed "in himself a self-sufficiency," and that his being and blessedness are one and the same thing. As a result of this pretending he is now never genuinely happy.

In this light and on the level of political theory, Jefferson's principle of the sovereign present could be both an implementation and an inflection or derogation of the Biblical notion of the presentness of the sovereignty of God. It is relevant to note that while Tocqueville observed that "among democratic nations each generation is a new people," by 1850, according to the *Literary World,* "anybody makes a new religion nowadays, a patent Christianity."[10] One might wish that every generation were a new people because religion would renew itself and, consequently, would renew the contemporaneity of its relevance. It is to be feared that, on the contrary, religion today is accommodated to the exigencies of the social and economic situation. Therein dwells the beginning of a mass-tailored religiosity.

The Social Gospel and the Acculturation of Christianity

The third feature to be considered in tracing the part that Christianity as a whole (and not American Protestantism alone) played in its own

secularization is the religious and economic composition of the Social Gospel movement of the end
of the nineteenth century. The optimistic progressivism of the nineteenth century had not blinded
quite all Christian leaders to the imperious necessity of coping with poverty and economic injustice. With different emphases but with a similar
concern, outspoken exponents from many lands
and divers confessions called for a social and economic awakening within the Christian churches.

In America, the Social Gospel took the form of
theological adjustments to the liberal mind. In a
way, it became the counterpart of the earlier and
more rigid Millenarianism. Whereas the latter had
relied on the propositional truths of orthodoxy, the
Social Gospel depended on the liberal postulate
according to which, ultimately, religion and culture are identical realities.

The Social Gospel conceived itself as the crown-
ing stage in the development of Christianity. It
regarded itself as the evidence that Christianity
was the only religion able to cope with problems
different from those of previous generations, both
internally (in terms of the so-called Christian culture) and externally (in terms of a more and more
direct confrontation with non-Christian religions
and cultures). The Social Gospel went further, in
affirming that Christianity was quite ready to
adapt itself to new conditions. One of its spokes-
men, Josiah Strong, wrote in *The New Era*, which
he appropriately subtitled *The Coming Kingdom:*
". . . evidence that Christianity is the absolute and
final religion is found in its power of adaptation

(29)

by which it has adjusted its methods and outward forms to changed conditions. Christianity has already had three great transitorial periods, and is now passing through a fourth."[11] The first three periods are early Christianity, the Middle Ages, and the Reformation. In the new era—Strong's book was published slightly before 1900—"Christianity will present a fourth new phase, the result of another adaptation to changed conditions; and this new phase, like the great Reformation to which it is complemental, will be both a return and an advance—a return to Christ's teaching concerning man's relations to his fellow-man, and an advance in the application of Christianity to *the organized life of Society.*"[12]

The two foci of the new Reformation are, according to Strong, personality, or an emphasis on the worth of the individual, and the organization of ecclesiastic and religious resources to fit the needs of the emerging situation. The first consists of a continuation of what had been accomplished since the inception of Christianity. Strong, however, who knew only too well how extremely individualistic Protestantism had become, attempted to stress those aspects of the Christian doctrine about man that would curb individualism. In his concept of personality he showed that human dignity is diminished whenever man neglects his participation in and responsibility toward the community.

The second focus—unbelievable as it may sound—was an anticipation of the modern organization as well as the organization man. From Strong's point of view, organization was the only means by which Christianity could hope to measure up to the task of the nascent century. Along with extreme Protestant individualism, "congregationalism" or denominationalism now belonged to a past epoch. Strong was in favor of "institutional churches" (such as the Baptist Temple in Philadelphia), which he considered thoroughly prepared and equipped to tackle the multitude of social and economic problems created by the exodus from the country to the city. In Strong's view this new Reformation was to be a completion of that of the sixteenth century. The completion was needed because, in the interval, the steam engine had been invented and industrialization had brought about the urbanization of life. The old individualism, while it promoted industry, in both the moral and economic sense, was no longer adequate to cope with the exigencies of an urban and, by definition, communal or, rather, collective life.

Reading Josiah Strong's diagnosis and his prognostication is more often than not merely a pastime; yet it illumines one's perception of man's nature and his religiosity, even though it makes one wonder whether the religious hope is not just one grand illusion. The significant fact is not simply that the Social Gospel hoped to establish the Kingdom of God on earth; rather, it is that Josiah Strong claimed that his diagnosis and his prognostications were scientific and based on objective facts. His works abound in charts and statistics, reflecting his constant and confident inclination to equate science with Christianity.

The dream of establishing God's Kingdom on earth was the result of a new and vigorous apprehension on the part of Christianity of its responsibility and relevance to the emergence of a new culture. It revealed an attempt, long overdue, to redefine and relocate the social commitments of Christianity. The active pursuit of this dream was concerned with finding the best method of adapting Christianity to the patterns of an industrial and urban society, and of isolating and ascertaining its point of application to the dimensions of a new society. Alongside of a sincere concern about delineating a new *modus vivendi* for Christianity, a sizable amount of self-satisfied delusion originated this dream and made an outburst of expectations possible, at least on paper. This delusion captivated the etiolated religious imagination in three ways, leading to the triple vagary of an unbounded confidence in science, a naïve view of the relation between Christianity and culture, and last but not least, a belief in the self-evidence of Christianity's relevance to the new social situation. And at their common root there lies perfectionism.

Strong could not quite bring himself to realize that even faith can lose its salt, although he admitted that "the skepticism which is most dangerous to Christianity today is not doubt as to the age or authenticity or genuineness of its sacred books or distrust of the time-honored doctrines, but loss of

faith in its vitality."[13] He did not admit to himself
that people could just as easily claim they worshiped no gods as that they worshiped God. At the
center of his system, and inebriating his puffy
evaluation of Christianity's vitality, he lodged this
unrealistic, self-deluding confession that, though
materialism and evil could upset the applecart,
ultimately "whatever is essentially unjust or selfish
is anti-Christian, and therefore temporary. It will
as surely pass away as Christ and his Kingdom
shall abide."[14] Strong based his assurance that "it
will pass away" on this expectation, as firm as it
was misguided: "Twentieth century Christianity
will instruct the social conscience, will teach that
the Kingdom of God fully come in the earth is the
true social ideal."[15] Contrary to Strong's Pollyan-
naish view, twentieth-century Christianity has
shown readiness to comply with political con-
cordats and crusades of all kinds, and one cannot
be sure that the major reason has not been self-
interest, direct or indirect. On another level, it has
merged with the democratic ideal.

But this picture of the Social Gospel is not complete. It does not account for the incalculable
amount of unrewarded and unselfish energy with
which its representatives coped on the practical
level with the inhuman situations created by an
industrializing society. A few of the leaders were
men of vision who achieved more in diminishing
the actual effect of the social problem than one
would surmise from their idealistic writings or
utterances. And not all the theoreticians of the

movement were under the spell of airy hopes. Its most ardent protagonist, Walter Rauschenbusch, was beyond any doubt the most sober in his dreams if not in his optimism. For him "the idea of the Kingdom of God reawoke with the rise of modern democracy." And though emphatically "now is the time for it," the idea of the Kingdom of God is not to be "identified with any special order." Basically, "it means justice, freedom, fraternity, labor, joy. Let each social system and movement show what it can contribute." Rauschenbusch wanted "the old ideal defined in modern terms."[16]

He believed not only in redefining the old ideals, but in implementing them. Underneath it all lay the supposition that these ideals were still alive and, socially and economically speaking, susceptible of programmatic translation and realization. The idea of progress was the moving force that could propel in one direction—or, to change the metaphor, gird together—all the modern equivalents of the old idea, namely, "justice, freedom, fraternity, labor, joy." Like all the others, Rauchenbusch expected that humanity would become better and better. Unlike them, however, he believed that it *should*.

Beyond the immediate human tasks and concrete responsibilities it assumed in displaying an almost prophetic consciousness of the urgency of the situation, the Social Gospel did not resist its Romantic inclination. This was as ironic as it was incongruous. In contrast to the German Romantics of literature, who fashionably if not unanimously lived off nostalgic representations of the Middle Ages, the Social Gospel eagerly looked forward to a golden age of its own kind. This was due perhaps to the fact that it drew its inspiration from Protestant sources. Unlike Rousseau, but like Nietzsche—two products of Protestantism—it regarded culture as an improvement over man's natural state. But like Rousseau, the Social Gospel was aware that men were still in chains, while unlike Nietzsche, it anticipated a steady amelioration of humanity. Nietzsche deserves praise for not developing his logic to the end, and for not accepting the idea of a gradual advent of the utopian society that would result from the cultural refinements of man's natural state. For Nietzsche as for Biblical thought, the relevance of the prophets does not lie in the realization of the ideals they proclaim. For them the authenticity and power of these ideals remain independent of their execution, even while they must culminate in action.

The radical utopianism of the prophets and the early Puritans was of a quite different nature from the utopianism of the Social Gospel. The first was realistic, the second, speculative. The ideals and imperative mandates of the former did not expire with their implementation, because they did not indicate goals but points of departure; they did not indicate what the Kingdom of God was like, but they pointed to God as the Origin and Fulfiller of history. By contrast, through the Social

Gospel programs, Christianity was perishing of its own realization.

The speculative utopianism of the Social Gospel, once it withered away, was replaced by pragmatic concentration on the calculable goals of an immediate future. The focus was altered. From Biblical radicalism, with its realistic appraisal of the human condition, of man's capacity for justice and his inclination toward injustice, the focus has shifted to a cultural and civic religiosity which inherits the mood and the letter but not the spirit of that radicalism. Secularism is the result of such a transformation. Biblical thought defines the secular as the area where, through action, faith in a transcendent God must show its relevance. Secularism, dishabilitating the act of faith, concerns itself with the area of action for its own sake.

Max Lerner has observed that, despite its individualism and anti-authoritarianism, and despite its concern with sin and salvation, the American tradition is secular.[17] At times it gives abundant evidence that it has succeeded in the acculturation of Christianity. It wallows, often with an amazing sense of prelapsarian sinlessness, in the immanentist worth and goods of the civilization it has fostered. Bible-reading (or its equivalent) and private judgment—both civic acts—neither affect society in a theonomous direction nor prevent salvation-minded men from cultivating prudent habits. As Reinhold Niebuhr would say, moral men do not necessarily constitute a moral society. Equally pertinent is the report of the Hoover commission, which stated that "the most fundamental change in the intellectual life of the United States is the apparent shift from biblical authority and religious sanctions to scientific and factual authority and sanctions."[18] The congruence of Christianity with the American tradition and the activism of American Christianity indicate that the latter has adapted to the results and consequences of this shift or, rather, this leveling down which distinguishes our age from the past.

Further Symptoms of the Dishabilitation

Christianity has sought to justify itself in the sanctioning of one political or economic order after another. Often this adaptation has been euphemism for expediency, and the price paid for adaptability has been a progressive if not always obvious dishabilitation.

Christianity sanctioned the feudal system of the Middle Ages (and to some extent reflected it even in its theology, particularly in Saint Anselm's theory of salvation, in which God, playing the rôle of a nobleman over against man as vassal, can receive "satisfaction" for man's offense against him only from his own equal, or Jesus the Son of God, since none but the suzerain could make up for the wrong done by one of his vassals to another nobleman). Again, in the name of religion, ethnic groups were sanctioned, in which one can discern incipient forms of nationalism, even though everybody lived under the banner of a common Christendom. Just as eagerly, Christianity subsequently promoted the virtues of the *bourgeoisie;* and today, when it does not actively or fanatically spearhead the crusade against godlessness, atheism, materialism, totalitarianism, etc., it becomes an all-too-prudent Good Samaritan, much too eager to help underdeveloped areas.

Christendom never actually existed even during the Middle Ages. For then, as any time before or after, Christianity was only too willing to compromise with the secular order. Certainly, in the Middle Ages the Roman Catholic Church clung to the theory that the state was the secular arm of Christendom, in the framework of which the Church represented the Kingdom of God. It is significant that the idea of the Kingdom of God was then restricted to the geographical boundaries of Christendom. It is as if the Kingdom of God would expand only if the boundaries could be extended. It did not, and this was not because Christianity was not ready to send out missionaries but because its interests were allied to those of the nations that made up Christendom. While diplomatic emissaries had reached Asiatic governments, no need was felt to send out missionaries. The Christianization of the world was largely conceived as dependent on the degree to which the Kingdom of God was coextensive and coeval with the European nations.

A few centuries later and *mutatis mutandis,* Josiah Strong wrote that "he does most to Christianize the world and to hasten the coming of the

Kingdom who does most to make thoroughly Christian the United States."[19] In either case, medieval or modern, the idea of the Kingdom of God developed a spirit of nationalism. Even more concretely, Strong had visions that the final dawning of the Kingdom was to be the work of the Anglo-Saxons. His reasons were that Continental Christianity was becoming weaker and weaker, while the Anglo-Saxon world was alone possessed of the missionary spirit, which he considered the essence of Christianity. Nothing, he thought, could resist this missionary spirit, just as the Mediterranean basin earlier was overcome by the Hebraic spirit of pure monotheism. Indeed, the world did not resist the Christian missionary spirit so long as it could not resist European colonialism. And even though "the policy of the East India Company was dictated by the most sordid selfishness," Strong (who probably was not alone) rejoiced that "it was providentially used to introduce Christianity and Western Civilization into the heart of Asia."[20] The vision of the Western people was so myopic that when Oriental traditions crumbled under the impact of mercantile self-interest, this was interpreted as a sign that Christianity was dissolving age-long superstitions and even shattering traditional religions such as Buddhism and Islam.

Easily and blindly, Christianity was wont to take the credit. But it did not realize that the Oriental faiths were temporarily disintegrating, not by reason of the self-evidence of Christianity, but

(39)

because Western governments imperialistically intervened on behalf of Christian missions. The treaty of Tientsin was signed over the selfish protests and in spite of the hostility of the East India Company, which until its dissolution in 1858 prospered on the superstitions of local peoples. The truth is, however, that Christian missions would not have been so self-confident were it not for the secular powers on which they relied and which they represented. It is a historical fact that, besides opening more ports to European trade, both the treaty of Tientsin, in 1858, and that of Peking, in 1860, also guaranteed the toleration of Christian missions and especially stipulated their protection. Expediency even entailed the patronage of France over all Roman Catholic missionaries and their activities.[21] Undoubtedly, this privilege accorded France a kind of subtle imperialism. Even anticlerical governments which at home harassed the Roman Catholic Church scrupulously exercised the privilege of protecting it abroad—not for the sake of spreading the gospel, but to gain political prestige and strengthen and expand their hegemony through the missionary network. And Christianity willingly made itself dependent on secular power to impose itself on Asiatic cultures. The treaty of Berlin opened the doors of Asia Minor to Protestantism.

From favor to imperialistic favor, Christianity reached the four corners of the world during the nineteenth century. This was a century of Christian optimism and missionary prosperity. Optimism and prosperity deluded Christianity into regarding its truth as self-evident. It should have been obvious that Christianity was dominated by the provisional supremacy of Western culture; and that this supremacy was derived from the technological progress that suddenly overtook an immemorial style of life which until then had still been informed by a supernaturalistic frame of reference. But, except for the orthodox party which saw in science a tool of the devil, the liberal-minded Christian approached the scientific and technological progress as a blessing of God's providence and joyfully invested it with confidence. In fact, he regarded it as "another table of the divine law given to man to meet new needs of civilization and to hasten the coming of the Kingdom of Heaven on earth." He believed that such a revelation of the divine law had already begun, as evident in the impetus Christianity seemed to receive from science. "This new evangel of science," wrote Strong, "means new blessings to mankind, a new extension of the Kingdom. The church ought to leap for joy that in modern times God has raised up these new prophets of his truth." Heaven was thus brought down to earth. Even the Will of God became scientifically accurate. The civilized society of the future, now discernibly irresistible, would be its ultimate incarnation. "The world is about to enter on a new era, for which the nineteenth century has been the John the Baptist."[22] And what Judaism and Jesus did to the Western world of antiquity, science and the missionary spirit would accomplish for the benefit of the whole world.

It is curious that those who dreamed of a worldwide organization of society always assumed that Christianity would be its main instrument and relied on science to destroy the superstitions of heathendom (including, to be sure, the few that linger within Christendom itself). Meanwhile, empirical and pragmatically rational, the scientific mind was actually undermining the Christian faith. The authority of faith was being devalued slowly and subconsciously. This was evidenced not only by the growing desuetude of the supernaturalistic elements of the Christian tradition, but also by a hardening of that tradition.

In the eighteenth century, Voltaire called England the most irreligious country in the world. Though this was perhaps an overstatement, Voltaire realized the nature of the symptom, because by "irreligious" he meant the movement of anti-supernaturalistic and empiricist reinterpretation of religion. As time went by, this trend increased and was accentuated. But the empirical immanentist approach was not exclusively the calamitous fabrication of deists. It was also adopted and fostered by intemperate proclamations in the name of faith. In the following century, for example, while the revivalist Charles G. Finney was suggesting that Jesus Christ should be elected president of the universe, the Vatican Council of 1870 proclaimed the dogma of papal infallibility with regard to *ex cathedra* statements about faith and morals. The devaluation of Biblical authority not only led to the secularization of religious ideals and practices; because of the devastating objections brought forth by rationalism, it also led to a stiffening of hierarchical Christianity and to the infallibility of the Pope as interpreter *par excellence* of a tightened tradition.

It is true that the doctrine of papal infallibility came about by virtue of an ultra-montanist show of force, over the opposition of the conciliar party. Nevertheless, this development represents as much the logical extension of Catholic ecclesiastical tradition as the usurpative substitution of the hierarchy for the tradition itself. Henceforth the tradition was no longer open to intellectual and historical investigation. It no longer asserted itself by virtue of its inner relevance to the contemporaneous situation. It was now controlled by authoritative and opportunistic declarations or directives. It became paralyzed by its subjection to the prerogative of a human office.

The dogma of the Immaculate Conception was, in 1854, proclaimed in spite of the weight of tradition and the authority of Thomas Aquinas, Bernard, and Innocent III. Ten years later the Syllabus of 1864 justified all the past, including such acts of the church as inquisitions and massacres.[23] At the same time, Roman Catholicism was explicitly tying itself with the medieval form of culture, refusing to acknowledge any merit in the idea of constitutional authority or that of the separation of church and state or even that of freedom.

It is ironic that the Pope should become infal-

lible at a time when Western culture was showing
many a sign of the death of God. For if, during
that period, the existence of God had implied a
devaluation of human existence, it did not follow,
as Nietzsche feared, that his death would alter
this devaluation significantly. Actually human existence was devalued even further, if one is to
judge by the prudentialism of Protestant secularism or by the opportunism of Roman Catholic
secularism. In both cases, compromise or self-
preservation overruled not only history and tradition but also faith in the transcendental presence
of God. And the atomism of Protestant self-seek-
ing individualism finds a counterpart in the singular atomism of papal infallibility. The sovereignty
of the present is their common denominator.
Ernst Troeltsch was right in observing that
Protestantism is but a modification of Catholicism. They raise the same questions, but differ in
the formulations of their answers. Both equally
can endorse a civic religiosity, like Roman religion, which adored the state, as Father Weigle
remarks, and unlike ancient Israel, which though
a nation, did not adore the nation.

In 1911, Ernst Troeltsch published his mag-
num opus, *The Social Teaching of the Christian
Churches,* which has become a landmark in the
history of Christian thought. A work of patient
and illuminating analysis, it carefully endeavored
to show both the influence of Christianity on
Western culture and the former's dependence on
the latter. Avowedly, Troeltsch was concerned

(44)

with the social teaching of the churches; however, our perspective of recent history and especially the support of his own later writings make it clear that he was also reviewing the relevance of Christianity throughout the ages.

He regarded the present century as a period of transition, but not of transition into higher spirituality or higher culture. On the contrary, he considered the prophetic and radical individualism of Christianity as "an interlude between an old and new civilization of constraint."[24] This, he felt, would soon come into evidence. In order to stress the past vitality of the Christian tradition and its problematic relevance in the period ahead, he compared the present situation with the process of dismantling a house and reutilizing some of its stones to build an entirely different structure. Troeltsch could not say what the new house would look like. He could not tell what relevance Christianity would have or if it would be able to show its validity. He hoped that Christianity would still take part in the shaping of this new culture, but added that "it will have to share the labour with other builders, and like them it will be restricted by the peculiarities of the ground and the material."[25]

The last clause is particularly revealing, because the word that ultimately sums up his study of the Christian influence on social ethics is *compromise*. The history of Christian social thought is the history of compromise. "It is, in the long run, a tremendous, continuous compromise between the

Utopian demands of the Kingdom of God and the permanent conditions of our actual human life." Troeltsch made this statement, twelve years after the publication of his major work, in a lecture on "Politics, Patriotism, and Religion" at the University of London. Then he added this ambiguous afterthought: "It was indeed a sound instinct which led its founders to look for a speedy dissolution of the present world-order."[26] It is as if the absolute otherworldliness of early Christianity, the relative otherworldly dualism of the Middle Ages, the unreconciled dualism of the Lutherans, and finally, the this-worldly or world-facing character of the Calvinist tradition had all resulted in the irrelevance of Christianity. Because, *ab initio*, they had to.

In 1912 Troeltsch had expressed thoughts which went to the core of this problem. Ready to discard the traditional forms and supernatural vestments of Christianity, he was trying to determine the point of a new Christian departure. He would not fully concede that the essence of Christianity had exhausted itself, if only because it was bound neither to its authoritarian church-type manifestation nor to its sectarian or mystical variations. He saw the possibility of a new type of Christianity, clearly distinct from either church or sect. Still, he was wondering whether this really was a lively possibility or just "the last echo of the Christian faith in process of dissolution."[27] Numerous difficulties, he thought, arose in the way of this new Christianity. Of the several con-

(46)

flicts it faced, the chief one was the necessity of safeguarding the person and the rôle of Jesus, without whom Christianity ceases to be. And yet, Troeltsch admitted, once anthropocentric and geocentric theories are abandoned, it is difficult to make room for the idea of a world redeemer. Troeltsch realized the depth of the conflict and its ultimate results. Faithful to the spirit of compromise he had studied at great length, he both affirmed and denied the distinctive elements of Christianity. That is to say, he would regard Jesus as a revelation of God, which lifts us up, well above our ordinary level. He would stress this image of Jesus and his testimony, particularly because it had been reinforced by the witness of several centuries. Only, one thing must be renounced—the belief that Jesus is the center of the world and the center of human history, for neither his uniqueness nor his significance consists in that.[28] Whereupon, Troeltsch consoled himself with the thought that the world is, today no more than at any other time, without God. But this is a confession of faith, a deeply religious conviction. Were it not for the respect with which he is regarded, one might say that this conviction simply prevented him from hearing "the last echo of the Christian faith in process of dissolution."

The great ages of the past have spent themselves, each in its turn. Some were ages of faith. The challenge of the Christian faith was sufficiently valid and relevant to radically transform the lives of men and their culture. Montesquieu could remark that, though Christianity was thoroughly otherworldly in its essence, it had had the greatest impact on *this* world. (From this observation, Montesquieu inferred a proof for the superiority of Christianity.) Outside of the Fundamentalists and other orthodox Christians, no one would at the present time define Christianity in terms of such a thoroughgoing otherworldliness. Christianity has become so this-worldly that, perhaps, it has lost heaven and this world, too.

CHAPTER III

Misbegotten Revival

DESPITE the overt proselytizing religiosity of our present culture and society, we live in a post-Christian era. People *try* God, or original sin, as others try the newest medicine. The historian Arnold Toynbee acknowledges this fact, while the Oxford–Cambridge Christian scholar, C. S. Lewis, ponders over the "un-christening" of Europe, particularly noticeable in literature, as the most important turning point since its christening.

At least three reasons may be brought forward to justify the use of the phrase "post-Christian era" to describe our time.

First, Christianity is today synonymous with religiosity. Its appeal to the masses is based on a diluted version of the original faith. The gap between the gospel and "the power of positive thinking" is greater than the one which, according to Tertullian (*c.* 160–220 A.D.), separated Athens from Jerusalem—pagan wisdom from Biblical truth. For the sake of easy consumption, the radical character of Biblical faith is diluted into re-

ligiosity: purely formal, innocuous, and somewhat
hygienic. The Christian vocabulary has very little
meaning for modern man except for the victim—
let us say, zealot—of religiosity. Religiosity is the
cunning by which secularism triumphs over faith
in God and, instead, sets up faith—faith in anything—as an end in itself. Such religiosity fulfills
civic ends: today it is socially fashionable to be
religious. Religious observance has reached an
all-time high; and religious affiliation has attained
peaks which Jonathan Edwards would not have
dreamed of.

Second, in proportion as Christianity is displaced by religiosity, it no longer inspires contemporary culture; its spirit does not impregnate
the ethos of our time. The modern world stands in
opposition to Biblical Christianity. The cleavage
between them becomes more and more grievous.
Nor does modern man look at all like any of the
Big Fisherman's contemporaries. Attempts—and
valid ones—are made to bring together the essence of Christianity and the realities of the modern world, to correlate the Christian answer to the
questions of modern man (as Tillich does, for example). Nevertheless, a sword of Damocles hangs
over Christianity. For the question cannot be held
back: Is Christianity—supposing that it has not
yet lost—fighting a losing battle?

Third, Christianity has lost its hegemony.
Whether spiritually or politically considered, this
hegemony, arduously established in the course of
centuries, is now disputed. It does not make itself

felt in international relations, except as it finds expression in the blunder of a diplomat inviting Jews and Arabs to settle their differences in a Christian spirit. It has already lost its scepter. It has lost even more on the national level—what with the coalescence of democracy with syncretistic religiosity, of which politicians, among others, speak eloquently and fervently.

An observation by Norman Birnbaum provides a starting point for the elucidation of these three statements. He once said that "the typical American today is, in fact, a Calvinist with neither fear of hell nor hope for heaven." A contradiction in terms? It would have been in another age. Today this description is significant in three respects, depending on what heaven and hell mean for this American. The first, the devaluation of Biblical terms and symbols, is the least likely, though a theologian would wish it were the most significant. Indeed, if heaven and hell rather literally mean "pie in the sky up there" and "gnashing of teeth down below," then no doubt the typical American is better off today, just as he is better off if heaven means a future life which deprecates and negates this life, and implies turning one's back on this world. The second respect in which this description is significant is therefore closer to reality: Norman Birnbaum's remark underscores the fact that the typical American's religion is a religiosity without marrow. The third implication hangs on the likelihood of the second; the average man is at once too religious and not religious enough. There is nothing surprising in that. The latent religiosity of every man has taken over wherever Christianity (seen here under the aspect of Calvinism) has abdicated. This religiosity is as shallow as it is intense, because it means that one believes merely for the sake of believing and because the Biblical terminology is foreign to man's self-understanding.

The concepts of heaven and hell are not so essential to the structure of the Christian faith as foes and fundamentalists alike claim. The Christian faith centers on the immediacy of God's transcendent presence in the world of things and beings. An understanding of this immediacy *today* requires other modes of thought in order to convey what the traditional concepts adequately expressed in a previous era. The faith does not hinge on those concepts, but on their content. The world of the New Testament, as Rudolf Bultmann keeps reminding us, is like a three-story edifice, since the earth is thought to be flat, lying between heaven above and hell below. New dimensions force us to correct ancient perspectives, though the question, "Who am I?" remains as central and fundamental now as then. Constant reinterpretation is a task which the perspectives themselves demand of every generation. This reinterpretation carries a danger—that of watering down the essential tenets of the faith, which are *independent* of their linguistic vehicles. The task is as difficult as it is urgent. It is difficult because no common language, religious or artistic, girds Western culture. It is urgent, because of those who clamor for a return to raw traditional concepts.

Paul Tillich's enterprise, a work of considerable scope and magnitude, is a unique attempt to mold a language consonant at once with the Biblical and traditional Christian symbols and with modern man's self-understanding. The nature, if not the method, of his undertaking recalls the work of synthesis effected by Thomas Aquinas in the thirteenth century. Tillich substitutes, for example, terms like "estrangement" for sinfulness and "courage to be" for salvation. But Tillich is considered an arch-heretic by traditional Christians, and is suspect by those—often non-Christians—for whom Christianity remains inextricably bound up with crude and rudimentary beliefs such as hell and damnation. In the world of Paul Tillich—that is, in our modern world—in contrast to that of Thomas Aquinas, there is no absolute. Ours is not only the world of relativity, it is also that of infinitesimal compartmentalization. And it is *infantile,* that is it does not speak a common language, if it speaks at all. It is a world of primeval, even primitive, religiosity. It defeats the well-meaning professional religious thinker. Followers of Tillich's modern-dress Christianity sometimes resemble those of Norman Vincent Peale, Billy Graham, or Bishop Sheen.

"God is a livin' doll," said the Hollywood actress turned Sunday-school teacher. This is a more damning pronouncement than Nietzsche's decree of the death of God. Increasingly there is a tendency, especially typical of popular but also of some highbrow religious literature, to emphasize God's love to the exclusion of the no less Biblical idea of God's wrath. How could a livin' doll be wrathful? No, we have not become more refined in our religious feelings and language.

We have domesticated God in such a way that, as *Waiting for Godot* seems to imply, he evaporates into a tragicomic mythological atavism; or he has become so diminutive as not to be recognizable any longer. To the actress's livin' doll corresponds Lucky's fractured existence and his broken mental record of self-understanding:

> Given the existence as uttered forth in the public works of Puncher and Wattmann of a personal God quaquaquaqua with white bear quaquaquaqua outside time without extension who from the heights of divine apthia divine athambia divine aphasia loves us dearly with some exceptions for reasons unknown but time will tell and suffers like the divine Miranda with those who for reasons unknown but time will tell are plunged in torment plunged in fire whose fire flames if that continues and who can doubt it will fire the firmament that is to say blast hell to heaven so blue still and calm so calm. . . .[1]

The play laconically takes note of the irrelevance, after twenty centuries of Christian influence, of Christian categories of thought and patterns of existence:

VLADIMIR: Do you remember the Gospels?
ESTRAGON: I remember the maps of the Holy Land. Coloured they were. Very pretty. The Dead Sea was pale blue. The very look of it made me thirsty. That's where we'll go, I used to say, that's where we'll go for our honeymoon. We'll swim. We'll be happy.[2]

Strangely—or perhaps not so strangely—what Estragon is yearning for is no different from the promises made to the devotees of inspirational literature, whether it is called peace of mind or of soul or "brilliant success" thanks to which "you will be gloriously happy."

The Bible speaks of the wrath of God. Some regard this as another aspect of the anthropomorphic nature of Biblical utterances about God. This is not wrong, but to reduce it to such terms misses the point. Biblical man yearned after happiness as much as modern man, yet he did not think that God lost his majesty because he could be angry. Rudolph Otto, in his book *The Idea of the Holy,* shows how in the Biblical writers' apprehension God is all that their anthropomorphic descriptions imply, and something more. He is love *and something more,* which the unexpected stress on his wrath intends to convey. At any rate, he is not a livin' doll. Such an un-Biblical familiarity calls for an iconoclastic retort like that of the French poet, Jacques Prévert: "Our Father, which art in heaven, comma, stay where you are." Not only has modern religion inserted a comma, it has also, with sweetness and sugar-coating nonsense, opened a wide chasm between God and man. The result is that religion looks more and more archaic, and even resembles magic.

But inspirational books are not alone responsible for that. Quite recently, the Archbishop of Paris, acting on behalf of the Vatican, reminded the priest-workers (priests who took jobs in factories) that they owe the Church unconditional obedience. Apparently some of them are still carrying on their apostolate, though it was forbidden by order of the Vatican. Like the heroine of *The Nun's Story*, they felt that the needs of disinherited men came before ecclesiastical routine and sacerdotal discipline. They did not look or act like conventional priests, but understood that if Christianity wants to preserve some degree of relevance in a society which is no longer sacral, the Church cannot afford the luxury of thinking that people center their lives upon it; they felt that the Church must be present where people work, eat, drink, suffer, kill time, or make love. The Church condemned their venture because these priests—as a Jesuit said of their fictional counterparts in some contemporary novels—seemed to act as though they were sent directly by God and were not ministers of the Church. In the official view, therefore, one cannot be sent directly by God and also be a minister of the Church.

Some years ago, Elio Vittorini[3] put the question even more incisively. The medieval synthesis, he observed, relied on Catholicism; bourgeois growth and progress, on Protestantism: How could Christians, he asked, concern themselves about the Christian quality of an age which is neither medieval nor bourgeois? "Technological" and syncretistic religiosity has begun to succeed Christianity. Does it have anything to do with Biblical faith? Obviously not, since one of the premises of technological or do-it-yourself religion is that it makes no difference what kind of faith it is. Religion thus loses its nerve. It also becomes more and more a civic matter, as it was in ancient Greece and Rome. American democracy is so religious that it would horrify the most Calvinist among the Puritans. Religion, like clothes, is mass-produced according to standard sizes: Protestant, Catholic, and Jewish. The Protestant Reinhold Niebuhr would not convert Jews; and Jacques Maritain, a Roman Catholic, in his social theory advocates religious pluralism so long as the social structure and underlying understanding of human nature are based on the recognition of an absolute (which, contrary to Pascal, need not be the God of Jesus Christ). Is it any wonder, then, that the agnostics and atheists and free-thinkers feel squeezed out?

The question is not whether Niebuhr and Maritain are right or wrong; or whether it is preferable to advocate a return to the past religious expressions and experiences, to the Catholic corporate society, or to the proselytizing zeal of Protestantism. Not only is this historically impossible; it is theologically undesirable. When the Children of Israel were settled in Canaan, the prophets kept reminding them of the unique experience they had lived through in the desert. What they meant was not a return to the social and cultural conditions of desert life, but that, *mutatis mutandis,* Israel should live in the spirit of faith in the true God which had enlivened it.

Our condition today is not very different from that of the ancient Hebrews. As the world shrinks, man becomes more and more of a nomad. This generation is one of displaced persons. Of course we don't pitch a tent now here, now there. But spiritual and geographic parochialism is no longer valid, much less tolerable. What happens in Algeria affects the United States; and what happens in the South is no longer purely local or national; it has diplomatic and international repercussions. And when it is our job that conditions the place where we reside, we are ironically more nomadic despite the routine of our provisionally sedentary occupation. Regardless of astronauts, we are nearer where we started from than we commonly think. Our religion is as crude as that of the fetishist.

Social, political, and international events have forced religious groups to tolerate and sometimes to borrow from each other. Contemporary society is a melting pot which eliminates not only national or ethnic differences but also religious affiliations, and its syncretistic religiosity is intensified by the pressure of international relations. The nascent ritualism of certain Protestant denominations may be a gain insofar as a *rapprochement* between Protestantism and Roman Catholicism is concerned. It is not a gain if the *rapprochement* depends on a loss of nerve in Protestantism. Similar remarks could be made about Catholicism or Judaism, for a blanket of anonymity is descending upon religion.

The resurgence of religious observance in the last decade hardly conceals the loss of hegemony suffered by Christianity. There was a time when Europeans considered Christianity the only religion. With the advent of the modern period Christianity became the "best" religion, especially when it was put in that position with the help of imperialist powers. Today the Continent has lost its prominence and America does not want to offend the parts of the free world which are not Christian. This may be why the fight against communism is envisioned as a Christian crusade: it is the only area where Christianity can proclaim its superiority without offending those who wield the power of international blackmail.

CHAPTER IV

Christianity, Secularity, and Secularism

Whatever the nature of its ingredients and regardless of its ambiguous purposes, the recent turn to religion in America has shown that religion and secularity cannot be separated. The unsophisticated masses have, through the crudeness of their religious gratifications, given a more real indication of how religion can speak to the present age than theologians or traditions have been able to exhibit. Such groping need not be inauthentic for being rudimentary. However superficial, however self-centered and hedonistic, this outburst of religiosity must be acknowledged within its limitations as a valid groping for an ultimate meaning. Regardless of the motive, the consciousness of a vacuous life is a sign of life-affirmation, or at least that the life more abundant is a possibility. Religiosity bears witness to this, and doubtless to the fact that the meaning of existence is a part of the reality of this world. Conversely, the religious upsurge of the nineteen fifties made it clear that the reality of the world is given with the fact of religious existence. This, when all the criticism has been piled up and sifted, may be a decisive gain. Should Christianity survive, it will have profited by the lesson.

Secularity as a Christian Obligation

To claim that faith is inseparable from secularity is not an innovation. Nor is it a reversal of the Christian tradition. It is a renewal, a reaffirmation, of the Biblical doctrine about the nature of this world and the meaning of the believer's presence in it. Essentially the Bible is not otherworldly in its assessment of religious existence. This interpretation fits the Old Testament more adequately than it does the New. But it does not violate the spirit of the New Testament, especially if one is to regard it as the fulfillment, not the negation, of the Old Testament—and one must do this according to the Christian tradition itself.

The Old Testament considers the world as God's creation and asserts that this creation was originally good, despite the fact that it also states (through the myth of the fall) that this goodness can be corrupted. Biblical thought considers the world as man's sphere of action and pre-eminence. Man's responsibility to God and his involvement in the world emerge as polar elements attesting to the original goodness of creation. This polarity never obliterates the possibility that the goodness

(61)

on which it rests may become self-centered or introverted. The locus of the polarity is at the same time a locus of tension. There is no dichotomy between man's responsibility to God and his involvement in the world, although there is a clear distinction. This distinction does not call for either man's withdrawal from the world or a separation between his religious obligations and his secular tasks. One finds in the Bible an implicit distinction between religious and secular, but the distinction does not involve a radical split between these two spheres. They are distinguished but not split or severed from each other. They complement each other in such a way that, as Martin Buber has said, the secular is not merely secular, but it is not yet holy. The distinction is between the religious and the not yet religious, or the holy and the not yet holy.

Because Christianity conceives of itself as the new Israel, the whole of the New Testament must be regarded in the light of the preceding argument, including those passages which seem otherworldly almost unmistakably. It is beyond the scope of this book to develop the various reasons for making such an assertion. Briefly, however, all religious language is essentially symbolic and not literal, much as fundamentalists and orthodox of all kinds would like it. And to say that it is symbolic implies that allowance is made for the idiosyncrasy of the culture and the class of people in whose language the religious truths are apprehended and expressed. For this reason, the various utterances of the New Testament which are spelled out in otherworldly terms must be interpreted in the light of the implicit coincidence between these terms and the fundamental concepts of the Old Testament to which they essentially refer. In other words, these otherworldly terms are themselves symbolic reinterpretation of the ancient Biblical insight, according to which man's involvement in the world, though not severed from his commitment to God, must not be mistaken for this unconditional commitment.

In the Biblical understanding of man's place in the universe faith, trust in God, and secularity could not be cleft from one another. This is what modern man has possibly discovered in the very ambiguities of his rather lowbrow religious search. There is no self-evident reason for denying him this, even though the supposed discovery is itself a benevolent and optimistic conjecture.

Historians have either accused Protestantism of causing the loss of the Biblical understanding of the reality of man and of the world, or they have praised Protestantism for the affinity it has had with the spiritual, intrinsic worth of the world as the *secular* "theatre of God's glory." Protestantism occupies a controverted place in the history of the Christian tradition concerning the Biblical emphasis on the necessary relation between faith and secularity. This can be studied from two angles. The first is an ecclesiastical phenomenon of routine if monstrous proportions, the repercussions of which have altered the course of Western history and culture: the sale of indulgences and Luther's reaction to it. The second angle is the Protestant understanding of human destiny and the spiritual quality of all human vocations, be they religious or secular, in the context of a culture impregnated by the Christian tradition.

Usually historians (both Protestant and Roman Catholic) have appraised the widespread sale of indulgences as a miscarriage of proper papal and hierarchical functions. The vulgarity of this pseudospiritual mercantilism cannot be defended from any point of view, even from the theory on which it was originally based. That theory dealt with the so-called Treasury of Merits, according to which the Saints had earned more merits than they personally needed to go to heaven. It was thought that the surplus thus accumulated constituted a treasury from which the Church could draw in order to help a deficient soul attain its goal. By the sixteenth century, instead of freely dispensing these merits according to individual needs, the Pope was selling them at what was purported to be only a nominal price. What irritated Luther at first was the greed, papal or otherwise, barely concealed if not openly displayed by such a commercial handling of salvation and the means of grace. But the result of Luther's initial revulsion was a completely different understanding of redemption and the signs of an authentically Christian existence. The sale of indulgences affected only the afterlife, and the Christian theory of redemption tended to assume more and more pronounced otherworldly connotations. Luther reversed this trend and assessed the validity of the new being experienced by man through redemption in terms of its relevance to his contemporary situation. The focus was shifted from the life after death to the life here on earth. So far as Luther was concerned no indulgence could be bought that would appease his conscience and alleviate his anguish here and now. That is the meaning of his theory about justification by faith according to which God alone is he who saves— and if he does so, he does it here and now. And that is why Luther had to broaden the medieval concept of vocation (which then applied only to the priestly office) to include all stations in life, whether lay or clerical.

Luther's conception of vocation, though broadened, was nevertheless static. This is shown by the Lutheran development of private and public norms of ethics and the subsequent division between the sphere of the church and that of the secular government. While such a resuscitation of the old dualism of sacred and secular is contrary to the spirit of Luther's theory of vocation, it is present in his basic distinction between the person and his public office. (Luther argued that a prince must govern *qua* prince and not *qua* Christian. The inertia of many Lutherans in the early days of Nazism was due to this factor.)

It was Calvin who recast the doctrine of vocation in conspicuously dynamic terms. His theory differs fundamentally from Luther's (and *ipso facto* from that of the Middle Ages). It holds that the Christian man must serve God—not only *in* the vocation that happens to be his, which means in spite of his earthly vocation; but he must especially serve God *through* his vocation. Whatever it may be, it is suitable for the glorification of God. Not only the minister properly glorifies God, but also the civil servant or the politician. No cleavage subsists here between a sacred duty and a secular one, between private and public morality. Given this premise, it is no longer possible to distinguish—except academically—the spiritual nature of man's commitment to God from the practical sphere of his actions and his involvement in the world. That is why Protestantism calls for *secularity.*

But it does not call for *secularism*—in which it has often resulted.

By secularity is meant the sphere of man's action. This means temporality in contrast to the divine eternity; and it means finitude in contrast to God's infinitude. Secularity refers to the ensemble of man's activities as well as his creativity, all of which reflect the Biblical fact that man is created in the image of God, but is not divine *per se.* Secularity also refers to the cultural manifestations of man's self-apprehension as a creature of God. Cultural manifestations include not only what is obviously such, for example art forms, but also ecclesiastical, theological, creedal, or liturgical forms. There is no reason why the latter should not be considered in the same cultural

(66)

category as the former. This is a reflection of the Biblical insistence to steer clear both of dualism and of monism—respectively, the separation and confusion of sacred and secular. For the Bible there is only one valid distinction: the holy and the not yet holy.

Once these characteristics have been understood, it is easy to distinguish secularity from secularism. While the former is that realm in which religion can show its relevance, the latter is an inverted or concealed religious attitude. Secularism is a form of religiosity, for which the present and the immanent are invested with the attributes of the eternal and the transcendent. It is an expropriation of religion, not for the sake of shaking off the tyranny of its supernaturalism as it is claimed, but really for the sake of another mystique and another fundamentalism or fanaticism. Few attitudes are more "religious" than those of certain secularists, who have deified democracy or sex or the classless society.

Protestantism and, indeed, Biblical thought are not compatible with secularism. This would contradict the basic understanding of man's nature as a creature, created in the image of God. And it would contradict the original Biblical view according to which one's faith in God and involvement in the world, or secularity, belong together. These two are united and can be separated only at the expense of one kind of fanaticism or another.

Modern religiosity looks like a curious mixture of Christianity, secularity, and secularism. The composition which results from these ingredients is rather amorphous. But it cannot be dismissed as being utterly artificial. No human situation ever is.

One thing, however, is certain. The alliance between religion and the world is ambiguous. One is not sure whether the revival has brought about a fresher understanding of religion in relation to the secular world or whether it has intensified and sanctioned an ill-disguised secularism. Some critics have wondered how it is possible to have a revival at all in the midst of an ever-growing and tangible secularism. These critics doubt that there has been a revival in any form or shape, except as a means of self-gratification. And chances are that this judgment is close to reality.

But there is another side, in the fact that modern religion, more self-consciously than ever before, has persisted in refusing to dissociate spiritual matters from secular realities. Faith in God has been extolled as a means toward wealth and success and toward economic and psychic stability. Faith and success and stability have often been literally equated.

Perhaps the materialistic equation that has been vulgarized and disseminated is a reaction against the un-Biblical otherworldliness by which Christianity has long characterized itself. This is a generous appraisal of the situation. In the main, emphasis has been on the pure and simple equation of faith and material realities. Secular motives needed to be sanctified because men will not forgo the goods that go with them. And why should they, unless it be for a clearly ultimate reason, which apparently is lacking?

Beyond the so-called secularism of contemporary religiosity, it is the lack of such an ultimate reason which needs examination. That, more than anything else, is the stumbling block of Christianity today. Material goods are not blameworthy *per se*. In many lands where the economy is poor, Christian leaders have often construed the task of Christianity as one designed to alleviate the suffering of the disinherited. No one can object to that. But there is a difference between people who are materially disinherited and those who are disinherited spiritually and seek alleviation through material means. Their spiritual poverty may well have resulted from an incapacity to endow material goods with a spiritual meaning. But they seek a way out, and no matter in what ways they look, at least they seek. It would be arrogant to dismiss even this kind of quest.

The Religious Revival as Secularism

Christian thought as a whole has never conceived the world as a place to be abandoned to itself, but as an instrument of God's glorification. From Saint Augustine on, this concept has consistently appeared in the history of theology. Augustine's vision of the City of God was his way of defining the possibilities of this world as a means intended for the glorification of God. And the classic expression of this view was formulated by Calvin's understanding of the world as the "theatre of God's glory."

On the other hand, the Biblical tradition has generally maintained that man is created in the image of God, but in such a way that God nonetheless remains imageless. God is not the sum total or the result of man's imagination. There is always a qualitative difference between God and man, as *intimate* as it is infinite. Similarly, man is to exert dominion over the other creatures and things of this world, but he must eat his bread by the sweat of his brow. All this suggests that the symmetry between man's obligation to God and his obligation to the world is never construed in Biblical thought as though it implied some cosmic harmony. This, from the point of view of the Bible, is where the Greeks erred. For the idea of a cosmic harmony necessarily leads to the doctrine of *ataraxia*, as it did when the obvious and inescapable disturbance of life shook up the belief in a well-ordered universe. *Ataraxia* meant freedom from passion, *i.e.* from soul-sickness, and (why not say it?) it meant mental health. Despite all the mental health strains of the modern revival and despite all the evidences of a cult of reassurance it presented in profusion, today's turn to religion does not entail any abnegation of material goods and values or of secular achievements. Certainly Norman Vincent Peale's version of Christianity does not call for a rejection of all secular abundance—quite the contrary. Material tri-

umphs are part of the modern gospel. Whatever
else it was, the revival of interest in religion was
neither Montanist nor Albigensian. It did not proclaim any radical withdrawal from the world. It
sought to attune, if not accommodate, the harassed conscience of modern man to the worldly
exigencies of his situation. (After all, was this revival not preceded by the Social Gospel movement and the secularization of Millenarianism?
Surely it must have benefited from both of them.)

The acceptance of the world fostered by the
present religious climate emanates from a quest
for harmonious consistency, from a nostalgia for a
golden age. Its understanding of the reality of the
world rests on another principle (*i.e.* the speculative harmony of an immanentally conceived cosmos) than that of the Biblical understanding (*i.e.*
the world as *God's* creation and the sphere of
man's commitment to him despite incoherence,
adversity, and evil).

The present acceptance of the world, and the
concomitant attempt to cope with the spiritual
problems this acceptance involves, are begotten
and shaped by a world-view fundamentally different from the Christian. The more Christianity has
transformed the world and made it more habit-
able, the more it has been unable to cope with it.
A well-ordered garden no longer offers the same
challenge as an uncultivated plot of land. No
doubt the world still offers a challenge. But it is of
a different sort, and it may take time to find it;
once found, it may call for an approach to reality

other than the one customarily prescribed by Christianity. The relevance of Christianity is being questioned, at least by implication, and Christianity is losing what relevance it had in the past. The conquest of nature may leave man with a certain feeling of wondrous triumph; but it is bound to be different from his previous wonder about its mysteries. Man may have thanked God for all sorts of natural resources; but technological mastery is bound to effect in man a different relation, or the absence of a relation, to God.

These characteristics give a strange appearance to the religion that has recently been revived. The strangest characteristic is that it has no historically recognizable identity. The religious revival did not insert itself in the Judaeo-Christian tradition. It was anonymous. It did not reinvigorate the contemporaneousness of the Christian message (or of the Jewish, for that matter), even if at many points it harked back to the past and the "faith of our Fathers." A transplantation is not a revival, especially if the soil no longer agrees with what is being transplanted. Atavism is neither growth nor strength. At best, it can display the appeal of magic; but this is neither faith nor commitment: it is escape.

There are three reasons for making these statements. The first and most obvious is the nondenominational popularity of the various leaders of the revival. Whether this is salutary or not depends on one's perspective. Some argue that the absence of religious partisanship is a good thing.

Even if this is admitted, the fact itself is important only in the light of motivation. And who can tell what a sound motivation is? How is one to determine the content of an intention, of an act? From a religious angle the objectivity of an action is even more precarious or hypothetical. It may be safer to assume that the disappearance of denominational rigidity was not due to any kind of ecumenical maturity as much as to a loss of confessional consciousness. This loss reflects the general deliquescence of the Christian faith. It is equally a manifestation of the entertainment value of the revival and their leaders. Protestants watched Roman Catholic Bishop Sheen on television and Catholics had to be forbidden to attend Billy Graham's crusade in New York.

The second reason is closely connected with the first. Religiosity in general, rather than the churches, was the chief beneficiary of the revival. Christianity, while it has contributed much to Western culture, is now unable to speak to it, nor can it profit from the crises of conscience through which modern man gropes for his soul. It is this religiosity more than any ecumenical maturity which enables interdenominational or nondenominational participation in religious mass events. Though it has been a long time since Christians were thrown to the lions, the principle has varied rather little: *panem et circences* has become *religionem et circences*. What else can a rich country ask for instead of bread? This is the irony of the time and the strange fate of Christianity—Chris-

tianity is swallowed up by the riches it has produced. When Jesus remarked that it would be
more difficult for a rich man to go to heaven than
for a camel to go through the eye of a needle,
perhaps he meant that religiosity rather than
riches would constitute a serious obstacle; and
that it should accordingly be difficult for a rich
man to be a Christian.

The problem has remained practically the same
since the days of Kierkegaard. As he saw it, the
main philosophical, or rather practical and existential, problem was, "How to become a Christian?" The acuteness of this problem was sharp-
ened by the fact that not only Hegel's predominant system, but also Christianity itself as an organization and a sclerotic mode of being, was
antithetical to the possibility of becoming a Christian. Kierkegaard did not consider the problem of
becoming a Christian as an adoption of one particular theory of beliefs or type of philosophical
system instead of another. He regarded it as a
singular mode of being in relation to God and to
one's fellow men as well as to oneself. He understood this mode of being as pointing to the task
of realizing in one's life the paradox of man's prox-
imity to, and his utter dereliction from, God. This
is what the Biblical concept of God is about. Religious existence is theonomous existence; but the
authenticity of religious existence is tested not
only by its fruits, but also by its roots. For Biblical
thought, the root of authentic religious existence is
God. The business of being a Christian depends

in a large measure on one's conception of God. This is not merely a matter of academic sophistication, but equally of practical relevance.

The last reason has to do with the various conceptions of God found in the pamphlet literature and other utterances through which this religiosity seeks to appeal to the masses. Modern man is not so much intent on inventing God, in case he does not exist, as he is on inventing concepts which, considering that they are only substitutes, are doing God's job as best they can.

Some of these concepts are plainly weird. God is referred to as a "Co-pilot" or a "Porter." Sometimes he is conceived as a Cosmic Pal. But all the time he is the nicest fellow one can ever dream of meeting. All those concepts have a common denominator: they all are anthropomorphic and they all originate in the inflationary imagination of sentimentalism. But whatever the theological or philosophical connotations may be, this anthropomorphism means that men worship the God they deserve. Men create God in their image. Their concepts of God represent but a hypertrophy of their self-understanding, and sometimes a pharisaic or moralistic sanction of their aspirations. Man's understanding of the deity is dependent on his highest values, and these are often created by his environment. God becomes no more than the ideal man.

Such a devaluation of God is not the monopoly of popular religion only. Nor is this negative appraisal merely the mark of a pessimistic approach to the complexities of human nature and its religious proclivities. It is corroborated in many modern novels. Studying some of these in *A Mirror of the Ministry in Modern Novels,* Horton Davies conducts his analysis in terms of five categories which also underlie the chronological development since Hawthorne. The problem that recurs in each of the categories is that of the relation between Christianity and culture. These two spheres, at the time of Hawthorne, are related and interdependent. Afterward, religion and culture go their separate ways, and the correlation of faith, knowledge, and science constitutes the next problem in a series of clerical portraits described as "divines in doubt." Subsequently, the priests of Bernanos, Mauriac, and Greene provide the sacerdotal approach to the problem. In the dilemma between religion and culture these priests are not much concerned about sacramental or liturgical obligations. The next category is that of the age of global expansion during the nineteenth century. Ironically, the novel of (or about) this period did not provide any estimable character. (Everyone remembers Sadie Thompson.) The last category is devoted to the present-day minister as community leader, wherever he has not been displaced by the psychiatrist, and where specialization (the mark of the age) permits.

Davies's book shows the unheroic worldliness of religion mistaken for a theonomous acceptance of the world. If it is not worldliness, then it is religion taking refuge in either sacramentalism or asceticism. As James Street said, "religion is nothing except humanity." It is the kind of humanity which is depicted by Black Wolf in Sinclair Lewis's *The God-Seeker,* which Davies cites. Black Wolf is an Oberlin-educated Indian who gives his view of Christianity in these words:

> Most of the whites believe, or profess to believe in Christianity, which is an idolatrous religion with many gods. Their Catholic sect has thousands of mysterious divine beings ruled by what they call the "Trinity," which consists of Father, Son, and Mother Mary. The Protestants have no Trinity, but a four-god council consisting of Father, Son, Holy Ghost, and Satan. . . . Among their demi-gods are Santa Claus, Luck (whom they worship by striking wood), saints, angels, seraphs, witches, fairies, vampires, evil spirits, the spirits of the dead, tombs and statues, the cross and a magic book called the Bible.[1]

To be sure, glibness about this matter may show mere smartness; it is not necessarily enlightening. This is a religious problem *par excellence,* since man everywhere is limited by the very words through which he seeks to transcend his limitations. In the Bible itself, God is referred to as a shield, as one who is "mighty in battle" and "teaches" the soldier's hand to war. He is paternal, even maternal, a shepherd, a friend, a bridegroom, a husband.

Why is it, then, that the modern ways in which popular religiosity designates God make one shudder? What is wrong with designations for

God as a "Porter" or the "Man Upstairs"? Why are such expressions more objectionable than certain Biblical ones which are no less down-to-earth and just as fragile?

It is not the modern phrase which can (or must) be objected to so much as the understanding it expresses of the self and its relation to other selves and the world, and to God. By contrast with the Biblical instances, these modern, popular appellations suggest that the deity is a missing link in man's unsuccessful attempts to grasp the meaning of his self and of the world. The deity becomes just a global hypothesis, a mere cog of an intricate machine, whether friendly or formidable. Thus the conception of God as the Cosmic Pal is but another step in the development of universal anthropocentrism, away from the original theocentrism of the Bible.

CHAPTER V

The Case for a New Christian Culture

THE claim is often made by some Christian thinkers that Christianity has not yet spent its full forces and that, accordingly, the Christian era is just about to begin. In view of the Biblical insistence on the correlation of faith in God and secularity, it is necessary that this correlation reflect and not disparage the actual secular reality and its structures. But this reality and its structures indicate the aspects of a culture modified by and dependent upon time and space. Therefore it is important that faith should understand its correlation to the secular as contemporaneity with it. Consequently, the problem dealt with in this chapter has two aspects: whether Christianity can be relevantly correlated with modern secularity; and whether modern secularity allows such correlation. Practically the whole chapter deals with Maritain's philosophy of religion and culture. This choice is dictated by the eminent rôle he has played within Christian and non-Christian circles.

(79)

Twilight or Dawn?

Whether a society is Christian or not can be determined by the extent to which its members practice Christianity. And whether a culture is Christian or not must be judged by the extent to which Christianity leavens its creative imagination. It is obvious that Christian practices have been abandoned or that men pay less and less attention to them. One interpretation of the meaning of this phenomenon is set forth by T. S. Eliot in his *The Idea of a Christian Society*. He writes: "A society has ceased to be Christian when religious practices have been abandoned, when behavior ceases to be regulated by a reference to a Christian principle, and when in effect prosperity in this world for the individual or for the group has become the sole conscious aim." But, Eliot adds, "a society has not ceased to be Christian until it has become positively something else."[1] Similarly, a culture has not ceased to be Christian until it is being positively informed by some other principle than that of Christianity.

But an increase in church attendance is not necessarily a positive indication of a revival of faith. Nor is the interest of the churches in the political or social situation of the world a sign of the vitality of Christianity. This interest may be born from considerations extraneous to the core of Christianity. It is not uncommon for a dying man to make one final affirmation, but that will not bring back life to his dismembered spirit. An example lies in the recent turmoils of the Belgian Congo. The highest rank reached by any Congolese in the security forces of that country was that of a noncommissioned officer. Obviously, the withdrawing Belgians had not done all they could to make easy the transition from Belgian to autochthonous administration. Despite these realities, a book on the contemporary situation of Catholicism published prior to the independence of the Congo praises the work accomplished there by Christian missions. It says that the Congo "is one of the most remarkable achievements of Catholicism" and, for this reason, "deserves a special mention."[2] Just what are these achievements? In the Congo 75 per cent of all the newspapers were Christian. Three motion picture companies are owned by Catholics, as well as one hundred and fifty-seven theaters to show these pictures. Add to these an equally impressive number of educational institutions, and it will seem that practically all the cultural activity of the Congo was Christian in its inspiration. The tragedy is that it was, but no one who in the summer of 1960 read the newspapers would have suspected it. To what extent is the fate of European and Western culture different from that of the Christian missions in the Congo?

As an organization Christianity lives on even under totalitarian regimes such as those of Eastern Europe. More is said and done about or in the name of Christianity today than in the nineteenth century. There is a closer affinity between religion and philosophy today, in spite of their clearer distinction and in spite of certain radically dis-

(81)

senting viewpoints, than there was at a time when Kant subsumed religion under morality or Hegel engulfed it into an abstract philosophy of history. In the field of arts, too, religion has in the last decade made a comeback, the importance of which far exceeds the spectacular publicity of the revival of the fifties. If all these signs cannot blindly be regarded as pointing to the vitality of the Christian tradition, can they be considered as an attempt on the part of Christianity to cope with the problems of the contemporary world? On what grounds is the claim made in many Christian circles that Christianity is today more conscious of its responsibility than ever before?

It is a fact that Christianity is today better aware of its obligation and that this awareness can be objectively substantiated. For example, nineteenth-century Christianity was essentially deprived of the sense of detached contemporaneousness. It lacked the courage to affirm itself in the midst of spiritual, economic, and social changes that could not be avoided and that should have been brought about by Christianity itself long ago. Even the Reformation, which understood the necessity that Christianity stands or perishes according to the degree of contemporaneity with the world in which it lives—even the Reformation acted as an instrument of cultural emancipation only insofar as it could not do otherwise. It was itself the result of a new phase and a new orientation in the national or personal consciousness of the peoples or individuals who held a common faith but did not see how this common faith in its traditional aspect could meet their situation. Today's Christianity is increasingly aware of the necessity to meet the present situation. More and more high-ranking posts (in the Roman Catholic hierarchy, for example) go to non-Europeans or non-whites; the World Council of Churches holds important meetings in non-Western countries in order to show the universality and, thereby, the contemporaneity of the Christian faith.

More decisive than these indications is the fact that in the realm of theology no emphasis is made which does not somehow concern the need for speaking to the present situation. Whether the particular label of contemporary theology be neo-Thomism or neo-Protestantism, it reveals an undeniable concern for a theology of immanence in the affairs of the modern world. Archaizing theologies do subsist, of course; they are unavoidable in any society.

Nevertheless, the question remains. Is not this need for contemporaneity an indication of obsolescence? The question is not cynical but very serious, forced on any analysis of the modern world by the observation that Christianity has traditionally been a religion of the future life no less than one which has sanctified its past accomplishments and has clung to them. Suddenly, it seems to want to be a part of the modern world and its destiny. It is natural that the basis of this claim should be questioned.

Although religion *must* be somewhat circum-

(83)

spect in its attempts at contemporary relevance, Christianity today again and again proves to be too hesitant, too cautious, too opportunistic in this regard. There is on the one hand a proud recollection of the praiseworthy ideals of the priest-workers of Paris in the midst of the proletarian mass of unchurched people; side by side with this commendation is a silence on the part of Catholic Christians, who praise only indirectly or privately the intention of this peculiar apostolic action, while they directly and publicly endorse its unjustified suppression by the Vatican.

So far as a feeling of relevance depends on the view that Christianity is the only real bulwark against materialistic atheism, the problem of today is not atheism but the progressive lack of currency of the Christian ideals. A passage of the act suppressing the priest-workers' activities states that no nation (such as France) where there are still so many baptized people can be considered de-Christianized. And so long as there are so many baptized people, it is not necessary to alter the traditional conception of the priesthood. Obviously, contemporaneity was measured by the persistence of time-honored practices and customs regardless of their present relevance or their actual irrelevance, in keeping with Eliot's claim that no country has ceased to be Christian until it has positively rejected the Christian principle around which society and culture have been organized.

There is a double fallacy in such an approach. The first is that it gauges the existence and the

(84)

vitality of the Christian principle in terms of traditions and institutions—and not in terms of a renewed confrontation with ever-changing realities. The second fallacy is that it severs morality and customs from the spiritual life, and cleaves culture from religion. Religion and culture are not the same thing, but though they must not be confused it is just as erroneous to sever them from each other.

Any cleavage between religion and culture, any dualistic approach to the problem of their relation, injures the vitality and relevance of the Christian tradition. Yet this is precisely the guiding thought of many who today approach this problem, from Eliot to Bonhoeffer and Jacques Maritain. After twenty centuries of Christian thought and influence these writers claim that the Christian era is just about to begin. They prophesy that henceforth Christianity will exert an influence equal to and probably better than that of medieval Christendom, admitting, with Christopher Dawson, that not even the medieval church quite succeeded in wholly Christianizing the heritage of Greek and Roman antiquity. Eliot eloquently states that Christianity has not yet fully spent its forces, but the validity of this claim in the light of contemporary events and realities can be examined more closely in the writings of Jacques Maritain.

A Christian Philosophy of Culture

For an examination of Professor Maritain's vision of a new age of Christian culture we must turn to his classical and most authoritative work on this subject, published under the title of *True Humanism*.[3] Although in this work Maritain expresses firm opposition to any kind of dualism, any kind of dichotomy between religion and culture, nonetheless he unconsciously slips into it time and again. For the religious and cultural pluralism which Maritain advocates is essentially a concealed dualism. It is a dualism which in effect is trying hard to fill the gap of nonsense left by the disappearance of a transcendent God.

Instead of concerning himself with this paradox, and instead of examining the legitimacy of the world born of the Renaissance and the Reformation, Maritain excoriates these two periods for what he regards as their half-truths and immediately asserts that today's struggle is principally centered on this alternative: either a purely atheistic position and action or a purely Christian position and *raison d'être*. Maritain is realistic enough not to favor the idea of a "return" to the Middle Ages, which he considers completely gone and unavailable for the present or for the future. Though medieval Christendom had the sense of unity, Maritain admits that the Christian ideals and the ethical demands of the gospel had not yet been purified, had not yet been grasped in their radical

(86)

exigencies, as they were afterward through the great upheavals and trials of the modern period.

But the modern period achieved the other extreme *vis-à-vis* the Middle Ages. While the latter strove after a sense of unity between religion and culture, the former exhibits an oscillation between a religious loyalty and a rather profane and sentimental naturalism. Not that the modern age does not display any humanism. It does. But this humanism is all too human. It is thoroughly anthropocentric. What Maritain seeks is its substitution by a true humanism, that is, one which recognizes both the existence of an Absolute superior to the order of the universe itself, and the supratemporal value of the soul.[4] Such a humanism Maritain considers basic and necessary to the creation of a new civilization. This civilization will be new not only by contrast with the "inhuman régime which agonizes under our eyes" and was fostered by the spirit of the Renaissance and the Reformation; it will be new especially in relation to the Christendom of the Middle Ages. By contrast with the latter, it will not be "sacral" but "profane."

The cardinal difference between these two concepts of civilization is felt more sharply if it is realized that while the medieval was not pluralistic, Maritain's is. This pluralism is held together by a common but minimum ideal, expressed thus: "Whoever is not against you is with you." For the medieval conception of an absolute end (namely the beatific vision of God), Maritain substitutes a practical concern for common action, regardless of the ideological goal, if that concrete action does not contradict the principle of an Absolute above and beyond man. With this as a cornerstone of his system, Maritain pays his respects to the necessity of defining Christianity in terms of the contemporaneity between faith and secularity and to the obligation to heal any cleavage between religion and culture, faith and morality.

This necessity and this obligation are all the more imperative because the future of Western civilization rests on a choice which, according to Maritain, lies between an anthropocentric or antihumanism, and a humanism of the incarnation or theocentric humanism. Maritain contends that the anthropocentric humanism of the modern period stems from the optimism of the Renaissance and the pessimism of the Reformation on the one hand. On the other, it is the legacy of a decadent *bourgeoisie*. Originally opposed especially to medieval humanism, modern humanism was seriously injured by Darwin and then by Freud, so that God becomes a mere idea, gradually deprived of any transcendence and ultimately bound to die or to be assimilated with the unfolding of history. Maritain has also in mind Nietzsche, Hegel, and dialectical materialism, or communism.

This kind of humanism is, according to Maritain, far from being rational—it is even opposed to reason. The tragedy of anthropocentric humanism is that it has resulted in tidal waters of irrationalism which are now sweeping Western culture under the name of racism and materialism. It is as if optimism is bound to lead to irrationalism as soon as it assigns a purely temporal destiny to man.

The Christian kind of humanism is not without some equivocal characteristics. In its Protestant trend it is still essentially archaic and reactionary, even pessimistic. There is a more Catholic trend which Maritain upholds, because it is "integralist" and progressive. Only this trend can usher in a new age of Christian culture. This new age would be characterized by three important aspects: a redefinition of the concept of man, centered in the idea or in the rehabilitation of the idea that man is a creature of God; a reassessment of culture and society which Maritain envisages as a transfiguration of the temporal order; and the necessity of tolerating heresies, that is, conflicting ideals, as long as they do not prohibit community of action —or as Maritain says, because *"oportet haereses esse."*

It is at this point that Maritain's edifice shows some weaknesses. He stipulates that this new age of Christian civilization must be founded on the distinction between the spiritual and the temporal orders, between religion and culture. This distinction appears to be in agreement with the Biblical view, but the agreement is merely superficial. It conceals a readmission of the classical error of dualism between heaven and earth, body and soul, together with the resultant dichotomous view of religion and culture. Maritain writes that culture is merely concerned with terrestrial matters, but the goals of religion are supraterrestrial and that such a differentiation is "essential to Christianity." Any attempt which presents the Christian faith in a mode susceptible to act as a leaven in molding the spirit of the contemporary world yet thwarts or belittles the intrinsic worth and the needs of that spirit is a sign of the inherent weakness of Christianity. In the light of this, the principles which guide Maritain's understanding of the relation between religion and culture and his hope for a new Christian civilization appear as falling considerably short of the necessities of the present age.

Turning, in accordance with the Aristotelian tradition of Scholasticism, to the distinction between the speculative and the practical orders, in *Art and Scholasticism* Maritain restates the two exercises of the practical reason: doing and making. The first deals with ethics and politics, while the second deals with "poetics," with the arts. One deals with moral action, the other, with productive action. The higher sphere of morality is the sphere of the moral virtue *par excellence*, Prudence. And what is the principal aim of morality, the main goal of Prudence? Maritain answers this question by saying that this "action . . . is ordered to the common end of all human life and it has a part to play in the perfection peculiar to the human being." The value of an act is related, even relative, to "the perfection peculiar to the human being." Action or morality thus simply refers to the goal of perfecting man, in contrast to making,

(90)

which is a kind of productive action "considered in relation to the things produced" only, and not in relation to the "common end of all human life." Productive action, that is to say, artistic and technical creativity, is related to the perfection, not of the maker, but of the thing made. In everything that is made, in every work of art, there are two elements: one is formal and the other, material. Controlled by the mind of the maker, the formal element is what constitutes each kind of art and makes it what it is. The material element, on the other hand, distinguishes the perfection of the thing made from that which is peculiar to the human being. Accordingly, it is not surprising that Maritain should acknowledge that "it is difficult therefore for the Prudent Man and the Artist to understand one another."[5]

It seems as if the respective exigencies of the two spheres of the practical order do not necessarily coincide, but granted that art and morality constitute two autonomous worlds, they are liable to enter into conflict regarding their respective perfection. In *The Responsibility of the Artist*,[6] Maritain tries to overcome this problem. Devoted to the ethics of Art, that book studies the relation between artistic creativity and ethical action in terms of the moral responsibility of the artist on the one hand, and, on the other, in terms of the perfection of the work in relation to the perfection of the artist's soul.

From the beginning, and throughout this essay, Maritain emphasizes the respective autonomy of art and morality. Neither is subordinated to the other in a direct and intrinsic fashion. However, an indirect and extrinsic subordination is allowed between them; its special purpose is to exclude any conception of art for art's sake, as well as propaganda art. While art for art's sake seems to vindicate the autonomy of art, it does so at the expense of the autonomy of morality. By contrast, propaganda art violates the autonomy of art. This means that Maritain's conception of the respective autonomy of art and morality does not rule out the possibility of their unity in the person of the artist. On the contrary, it is from this perspective that Maritain views the worlds of art and morality. And if these worlds constitute independent spheres, it is no less true that they remain concentric. Why? Because Maritain reverts to the strict Aristotelian distinction between the speculative and practical orders and observes that both art and prudence are virtues of the practical intellect. Nonetheless, the difference between art and morality remains. The first responsibility of the artist is toward his work. Maritain quotes Oscar Wilde: "The fact of a man being a poisoner is nothing against his prose." The end of art, which is beauty, is supreme with respect to the work, while the end of prudence, which is the Good, is supreme with respect to the man.

Therefore, when these two ends are conjoined in man, they form one absolute, which is the Greek ideal of the *Kalokagathos*. The artist is a man before being an artist; as such "he is responsible to the good of human life, in himself and in his fellowman." Maritain here declares that "the autonomous world of morality is simply superior to (and more inclusive than) the autonomous world of art." This assertion hangs on the principle that "there is no law against the law on which the destiny of man depends." In other words, "Art is indirectly and extrinsically subordinate to morality."

Evidently, everything depends on what is meant by morality. It need not be moralism and prudery. One might even find in Maritain's understanding of morality more than a mere possibility of accord with that of Albert Camus. By morality Maritain means essentially charity, just as Camus's description of "engagement" or commitment hangs on his concept of love. Both do in effect consider a strict union between action and art. But Maritain expresses this union in terms of the relation between the perfection of the work itself and that of the maker. Relying on Thomas Aquinas, Maritain defines perfection as the point when any being or any thing reaches its end. Thus, ultimate perfection means union with God, and such a union with God can only be achieved through charity.

It is here that Maritain leaves his theory open to the criticism that, though his understanding of perfection is based on charity, it does not quite refrain from depriving the object of this charity from any intrinsic worth. The fact that love itself, or charity, is defined purely in terms of a supraterrestrial reality can only signify that the union with

God is but the ultimate expression of an other-worldly hope: and it is questionable whether this hope can deal with the realities of this world otherwise than by asking man to renounce them. In the present predicament of Christianity in its strained relations with the culture it has fostered, one may wonder whether such an otherworldliness is opportune. Yet this attitude is adopted at a moment when, at least theoretically, most Christian leaders are conscious of the paramount need of contemporaneity, and when, seemingly, this effort to let Christianity keep abreast of the time is most conspicuous in every quarter. But, always, some kind of otherworldliness seems to dilute the reality and the effects of Christianity's encounter with the world.

This can be felt even when Maritain writes with apparent wisdom: "The most disincarnate artist has a concern, concealed or repressed as it may be, to act upon souls." As Sartre would say, no author writes for posterity or even for himself alone. Moreover, the work of art involves not only a technique but also the whole being of the artist—even of the artist *qua* man and not simply *qua* artist. Indeed, art depends, in Maritain's words, on "everything which the human community, spiritual tradition and history transmit to the body and mind of man," just as, because "art belongs to a time and a country," it has an obligation toward the community. Once again, Maritain's theory shows its defect. He grants the world of art its autonomy only to make sure that it subordinates

(94)

itself to the world of morality. Indirectly and extrinsically or not, the subordination is there and it is emphasized. It is morality itself which judges the quality of a work of art.

Maritain admits the possibility of a conflict between the "good of the work" and the "good and ultimate end of man." What must an artist do under such circumstances? Maritain's answer is unambiguous. He declares that "the only solution for such an artist is to change, not his work (as long as he remains what he is), but himself. Then his artistic conscience itself will require of him another kind of work." But what happens to the other work, toward which he is counseled to change? Is it still to be considered as art or not? Maritain's theory does not offer any answer. Why? Perhaps, because there is a gap between the Christian definition of man and the understanding of human nature which evolves out of the unhindered work of man's imagination. Maritain has not, despite his awareness of the need for contemporaneous Christian action, removed the barrier which separates this world from the next and Christianity from the culture of today.

In 1880, E. de Pressensé observed the death of Christian philosophy precisely because it then seemed to become a mere re-apparition from the thirteenth century. The mistake of Jacques Maritain is not that he believes in the reality of a transcendent God. It is that he does not dissociate this belief sufficiently from the supernaturalism peculiar to the thirteenth century. It is one thing to affirm that "man is an animal who lives on transcendentals." But it is another thing to affirm that the reality of immanentals participates in the power of the transcendent—or that the transcendent manifests itself in the immanentals only within the realm of the Christian church. By asserting that the church alone, as a temporal and social community, seeks and realizes a common good which participates in divine truth, Maritain deprecates the intrinsic worth of all other temporal community. Surprising as it may sound, this is the reason why he chooses to place the good of the work of art in a subordinate position with respect to the good and ultimate end of man. Maritain defines the perfection of the work in such a way that it is consubstantial with the perfection of the soul which every man, by virtue of being a man, must seek. In these terms, the artist must be a saint.

Maritain's positive approach to the independent reality of culture is but a pretext better to absorb it into the realm of an otherworldly reality, namely the Christian tradition. But he does not thereby salvage it from its increasing irrelevance, for if the artist must endeavor to become a saint, his art is superfluous. As Mauriac has said, if one were a saint, one would not write novels. Nor would one be a doctor, nor a politician nor, to use Maritain's own words, "anything here below, save perhaps a monk."

Maritain asserts the autonomy of art in regard to morality as well as its extrinsic and indirect subordination to the latter. This assertion leads to the core of the predicament of contemporary Christianity and its inability, even inaptitude, to speak to the modern situation. All that Maritain's theory of aesthetics, all that his religious philosophy of culture, achieves is to reassert, even if mildly, the old deprecation of life here on earth. Maritain, like many another Christian throughout the ages, speaks highly of culture and the arts; he is, even more than many another, concerned about their vitality under a Christian influence; yet his views reveal the same spirit of otherworldliness and contempt for this world on which centuries of Christianity have thrived. "I could have become a saint," said Léon Bloy, "a worker of wonders. I have become a man of letters." Here, as in the case of Maritain, there is more than merely a question of subordination which is involved, as well as something other than an intellectually legitimate attempt to correlate two realms of human existence —art and morality. In Bloy's statement, as in Maritain's theory, it is the implicit disparagement of the world as it is, of the intrinsic worth of the creation, which is shocking. It is a question, therefore, whether any rethinking of Christianity in contemporary terms can be relevant so long as no simultaneous attempt is made to dislocate and expel the habits of life-denial which have characterized Christianity. The problem is as simple and unambiguous as Marx expressed it: "It is easy to become a saint if one does not want to be a man." Father Paneloux's behavior in Camus's novel *The*

Plague is an illustration of that kind of ideal. To be a man—this is today's problem as it has always been. Neither Marx nor Camus have given it originality. But Christianity has tended to disregard it for the sake of a supernatural concern which is deleterious to human existence here on earth. Today's battle is not waged in the spaces between heaven and hell. It is fought within man himself— for or against him. That is the real issue.

Maritain's pluralism is a refusal to face this problem. The problem is further complicated by the fact that while Maritain acknowledges the skepticism of today's culture, he does not quite take it seriously. Indeed, "there is something disingenuous in the argument that a return to absolutes will eliminate skepticism."[7] In advocating pluralism, Maritain simply sweetens the pill. It is the diagnosis itself which is wrong. The loss of absolutes cannot be remedied by an edulcorated appeal to unidentified absolutes. Saint Thomas Aquinas's absolute had a definite identity which authenticated his system of thought and his beliefs. Maritain's absolute is neither a reference to the God of Abraham, Isaac, Jacob, or Jesus Christ. It suggests the god of philosophers, who have ceased to believe in any. Maritain's attitude is less courageous than that of Camus. At least Camus dared to draw all the consequences from the death of God, to the point of facing the absurdity of human existence and to the point of despairing until a new hope was born, until a new ethic was felt and sketched. In Maritain's system the disappearance of God is glossed over; and for lack of any affirmation of God's existence in the fashion of the old schools, Maritain either wishes that all our absolutes were summed up in his God or he does not refute the death of God. Maritain's absolute is an apparition. It shows that the predicament of a Christianity which attempts to be contemporaneous with its concomitant culture is even greater than one which does not care about it or declares itself purely and simply otherworldly.

Maritain himself realizes this difficulty. In *True Humanism*, he contemplates the new regime of Christian civilization as differing from the medieval one in that it would not be "sacral" but profane. But here, too, the distinction is merely verbal and does not affect the core of the problem. It offers no new departure for a new Christian culture, and thus offers no new and viable challenge. The passage from a sacral to a profane emphasis is not going to alter decisively the chances and the opportunity of a Christian culture. It is merely a question of semantics. Even as Maritain likes to speak of absolutes which distantly recall Saint Thomas's God, so also he favors—for lack of any other possibility—a profane culture which is but a substitute for the irretrievable sacramental culture of the Middle Ages, since no one can humanly hope to resuscitate the latter today.

What Maritain's cultural philosophy amounts to is a proclamation that things would be better if they were under a Christian influence. This constitutes a recognition that they are not. To advocate that a profane culture must be erected which would replace the sacral culture of the Middle Ages constitutes more than a *de facto* acknowledgment that the Christian principle is losing control of the cultural structures of modern society. It is one thing for a Christian to believe that the powers-that-be draw their authority from God; it is another thing whether the powers-that-be themselves believe it. Although a Christian could make his own some of Karl Marx's indictments of the bourgeois morality and economy, the fact is that Marx formulated them in a sense hostile toward Christianity. It is as if, throughout the ages, Christianity had learned less from its historic sins and mistakes than it reluctantly did from the attacks and corrections of its detractors. There must come a time when the detractors take over the leadership.

Maritain is unwilling to realize that his scheme for an integral humanism is such that it hardly conceals the influences of secular thought upon his own understanding of Christianity. He once wrote that the misfortune of classical humanism was that it was anthropocentric. The predicament of Maritain's humanism is that it deliberately wants to be profane but not anthropocentric. It wants to honor life and the world without deriving this honor from the intrinsic worth of either this life or this world. Just as he subordinates art to morality and thus honors it, so also he subordinates this life and this world to a supernatural reality and thus hopes to honor them.

Is this the kind of civilization Maritain wishes to see as a real possibility? Perhaps this is all that a Christian civilization can be in the future. But will it really be a civilization? And just how far or how different is Maritain's neo-Thomist civilization from the ideals of pragmatism? Is not what he calls pluralism another label for pragmatism? It seems that Maritain is only trying to save the concept of God by substituting for it the concept of an Absolute. But this concept of the Absolute is related to man or founds man's self-understanding in a way no different from William James's definition of God as the ideal of everything.

Such is the Christian humanism underlying Maritain's conception of civilization. This humanism, Maritain says, has been absent from the concern of modern man during the past four centuries. Now man has come full circle, realizing the nonsense of that inhuman humanism which was centered on man rather than on God. Maritain thinks that no new humanism is conceivable if it is not inspired by a Christian philosophy—a philosophy of the supernatural, of the emotional as well as of the supraterrestrial end of man. The "higher" the point of departure, the better this new humanism will inform, shape, and direct man's destiny in the framework of a long-needed new civilization. And, Maritain adds, from what height can such a humanism be derived? From the height of saintliness. It is not from the depths and the finitude and limitations of man's condition that Maritain derives his humanism. The culture he contemplates is not really addressed to

this man in *this* condition. His humanism is based
on the life of one who renounces life because it is
not good enough—and yet it is the only one he
has. Any culture based on such a humanism may
be Christian and even pluralistic, but it will essentially be programmatic and—because it is blind to
the limits and the possibilities of human nature—
it will be a counterhumanism, at least from the
present standpoint of man.

Maritain's philosophy of religion and culture reveals the presence of an ineluctable dualism at
its very base. This dualism permits Maritain to
separate religion from the cultural framework and
institutions of society; at the same time it permits
him to fill the gap thus created with the insertion
of an absolute principle in terms of which both
man and society are explained transcendentally.
The result of this dualism is an otherworldly conception of religion.

In a volume published in 1943 under the title
of *Sort de l'homme*,[8] Maritain includes an essay in
which he discusses the influence of religion on
modern society and culture. In it he clearly distinguishes the political meaning of religion from
its evangelical significance. What he means is
that the inner reality of religion, or faith itself, is
existentially more authentic than the cultic and
even charitable institutions by which religion is
often known—that the otherworldly focus of religion is more important than its this-worldly concern.

In the same essay, Maritain states his opinion

that the evangelical conception will ultimately prevail over the political conception of religion. Not that Christianity will no longer use cultic and social institutions; but it will be free from them, especially the latter. It will inform the temporal structures of the world, but it will not be a part of them. Thus, he adds, the idea of a Christian state is today very remote. The Christian states of the past have now become bankrupt— apparently because (or in spite?) of the fact that they were based on a political conception of religion. Though Maritain rejects the political conception of religion, he is compelled to avow that every Christian must wish for "the ushering in of a really Christian world order, or a really and organically Christian state, which externally professes Christianity." This hope is not anywhere near realization, especially today when the old Christian states are disintegrating and giving way to various forms of totalitarianism which arrogate to themselves the messianic visions of classical Christendom. How is it then that Maritain believes that a new Christian civilization is going to rise from the ashes of the modern world and from the constraint, the irrationalism, and the directionlessness of the present day?

Together with its dualism, Maritain's philosophy of religion and of culture nourishes a basic inconsistency. It is foolish to hope for a new Christian culture once Christianity has forsaken the temporal structures of this world. It is inconsistent to think that one can be had without the other. If any truth is to come from religion, it must deal with the present, this-worldly condition of man. Even Saint Thomas admitted that God had not for his own but for man's sake created everything for his glory. To be sure, in dissociating faith from the temporal structure of the world, Maritain intends above all to assert the primacy of the spiritual. It is evident that such primacy must always be asserted if any renewal, whether religious or cultural, is to be hoped for in a world torn between all kinds of ideologies. But such primacy must also show some efficacy in this world and for it. The primacy of the spiritual cannot be realized in and for this world in any other way—even if it must negate itself in order to be thus realized.

Maritain's insistence upon religious and cultural pluralism within the framework of a reinvigorated Christian civilization has many merits, not least of all the recognition of alternatives to the Christian faith itself and accordingly the recognition that all men belong together. But it would be a mistake to assume therefore that Maritain is attempting to reverse the age-old dogmatism and exclusivism of Christendom. It would be a mistake to think that this new version of a Christian culture distinguishes itself by its openness and an inherent attitude of tolerance toward heterogeneous elements. What Dr. Maritain's position clearly spells out is not the toleration of non-Christian elements. The converse is the case. Unconsciously, if not consciously, Maritain is presenting the fact that henceforth it is probably Christianity which will need the toleration of others. In accord with T. S. Eliot, Maritain, too, seems to think that "it may turn out that the most tolerable thing for Christians is to be tolerated." But being tolerated is quite a different thing from occupying a position of influence upon the structures of a profane civilization under Christian inspiration. When the kind of profane culture Maritain envisions comes to pass, it may be that Christianity, now merely a tolerated religion, will have ceased to guide the destinies of men. To borrow Maritain's own terms, the relation between Christianity and culture must be direct and intrinsic. As soon as it becomes indirect and extrinsic one is subordinated to the other. In the Middle Ages, culture was thus subordinated to religion. Whether Maritain likes it or not, and though he does not say it, his prospect is headed for the subordination of religion to culture. An extension of his own arguments negates his expectation that the era now beginning is to be characterized by any form of Christian dominance.

CHAPTER VI

Present Culture and Its Case Against Christianity

"IF God does not exist, everything is permissible," argues the atheist. On the empirical level of human existence, as Dostoevski's *The Brothers Karamazov* shows, the logical consistency of this thesis refutes itself. For, if everything is permissible, murder is a legitimate action and, consequently, suicide is the only authentic act. But life precisely contradicts this thesis. Therefore, the Christian argues, life is not an absurd labyrinth of permissible speculations about abstract acts; it is the unfolding, now bright now dark, now hopeful now desperate, now meaningful now meaningless, of a single action, namely, that everything is grace because there is a God. Thus the Christian states his position: "God is, therefore all is grace."

Modern man is the legatee of the Christian as well as of the atheist. He agrees with the Christian that all is grace. He agrees also with the atheist that God is dead. His argument is: All is grace, therefore God is dead. For if life is meaningless, then there must be no God. But, if it is meaningful—and it must be, or else it contradicts itself—it is meaningful by virtue of some kind of *immanent* grace; therefore God does not exist. If all is grace, then God is dead. Or: All is grace because God is dead.

God Is, Therefore All Is Grace

Jacques Maritain is too much of a Thomist to show any signs of perplexity or anxiety in his philosophy. Not that Maritain knows nothing of the despair, the cruelty, and the irrationalism peculiar to this age. But his confidence in the supernatural hope of his faith compels him to regard these as mere signs of a degeneration, of a fall from a period of culture impregnated by grace to one which can be but transitory. The degradation and shame of the present epoch is for Maritain sufficient proof of the need for a new Christian approach to the problems of modern society. He is firmly convinced that the structures of the new era can be built on Christian foundations especially redefined for this purpose. But his understanding of Christianity and his definition of its role in framing this new culture are so broad that one cannot help but realize the ambivalence of his conviction. Maritain is saying that so long as Christianity has not been positively replaced by another religion it will continue to exist. This is a truism. But so long as it continues simply to exist, it will merely be tolerated. There is a huge difference between the position of Christianity in Maritain's view and that of the early Christians. Maritain declares, "*oportet haereses esse*" ("there must be heresies"), while the early Christians were told, "*non licet vos esse*" ("you are not permitted to exist"). Whatever one wishes to make of this difference, it asserts that Christianity has lost its hegemony. All it can hope for from the heresies it must tolerate is to be tolerated also by them.

Christianity cannot hope to survive if it is opposed to life itself. It must compose itself to the facts of this world. It may well be that the frustrated expectation of the Second Coming entertained by Saint Paul's correspondence is only now coming to maturity and to fruition. The hope of an imminent Parousia implied the abandon of a concern about this world. Grace could be found fully only in the future life, not in this one. The obvious delay of the Second Coming forced Christianity to regard this world in a somewhat different light. Under the aegis of the medieval synthesis *grace* was defined not as the abolishing but as the perfecting of nature. This view did not quite eliminate the old contempt for the world vividly expressed by the expectation of an imminent return of Jesus. It simply subordinated nature to grace and created a scale of values between them. In this subordination grace is everything, but everything is not grace. Maritain attempts to say that everything is grace.

In the world of the novel this attempt seems to

succeed and become fully realized. There, too, the last palpitation of a Christian culture can be felt; to say that everything is grace often is another way of saying that the traditional Christian subordination of nature to grace is no longer viable. Tortured and sometimes eccentric if not despairingly hopeless, the novelist who is also a Christian shows that Christianity is unable to make sense today unless it protests against itself as against its own structures and its own achievements. Even if theologically speaking Christianity must protest against itself if it wishes to remain authentic, it is nonetheless ironic that this means that Christianity is to be found nowhere, not even within its own precincts. What many contemporary novelists are describing is Christianity's alienation from itself. This self-alienation creates no new act of cultural and social awareness except privately and individually. One must always begin with individuals; but individual Christians can change the world only if they are alienated from the world and if they are not self-alienated. They cannot exculpate themselves from the secularization of Christianity. There cannot be any form of Christianity-in-exile as captive peoples set up governments-in-exile. Rather it is to Formosa in relation to the Chinese mainland that Christianity should be compared in its relation to modern culture and the course it is taking.

Paul Claudel was a man of letters in whose inspiration Christianity took the shape of a glorified Formosa, always acting as if nothing had shaken the mainland of Western culture. Such writers *"se barbouillent de sublime,"* observed Georges Bernanos, *"ils se mettent du sublime partout,"*[1] forgetting that Christendom had more in common with the lowly and the disinherited than with the Renaissance palaces or with the imagination of those all-too-secular painters who painted the Holy Virgin after their mistresses. Inflationary Christianity is possible only when there has been a recession of faith; any exhibition is then received as a genuine expression of belief. This inflationary vision of Christianity has often resuscitated a Baroque style, especially in literature. Like the Baroque architecture of the sixteenth century, it is more of a concession to the forces of secularism than an instrument of God's glorification. Unable to maintain its identity in a world dominated by hostile ideologies, it pretends to ignore all hostility in the name of a love too zealous not to suggest the protest of a betrayer. To quote again Bernanos, "one does not lose faith, it simply ceases to inform one's life"; but people continue to act as if this has not happened.

A few novelists have realized the precarious position of Christianity in the struggle that goes on today to capture man's allegiance. Christianity is one among several rivals, and is reduced to the dimensions of an ideology. It is not less corrupt than the forces it tries to combat. In its appeal to modern man it presents its demands as easier to fulfill than those of its opponents. Modern Christianity has come considerably closer to man's desires and appetites than did traditional Christianity, but it has in the process degraded itself to the level of an opiate or that of moralism. Its god is easier to satisfy.

According to Bernanos, religion itself is the major cause of this corruption within Christianity. The Christian Bernanos analyzes the situation in the same way as Samuel Beckett. In both *The Diary of a Country Priest* and *Waiting for Godot* one is struck with the analogy of their revelation about the present state of Christianity. A sign of hope, from the Christian perspective, remains in Bernanos's novel, while it is absent from Beckett's play. But Bernanos's priest cuts a different figure from that of the ordinary priest in respects other than those that would come to one's mind. It is not the intense spiritual concern of a Bernanos priest which puts him in another category; nor is it his love for his mission and the obligations with regard to others this causes him to develop which singularize him. More deeply, it is his fight, not against the decay of society or the corruption of morals, or simply what would be called the world, but against Christianity itself. *Mutatis mutandis*, his struggle presents the same characteristics as that of Graham Greene's whisky priest in *The Power and the Glory*.[2]

The association of these two figures is not farfetched. Greene's priest is externally fighting against a pagan or anti-Christian organization of society. But internally he is not less concerned about the lack of spiritual resources within Christianity. His behavior is not merely the behavior of an odd priest whose eccentricity has gone too far. His addiction to alcohol is a weakness, perhaps; but it is also a sign of the need for a new inspiration. His illegitimate child may be a symbol of a moral aberration; it is also a live reminder that Christianity cannot go on self-complacently: it must begin again, start all over, especially if its spiritual reserves have been exhausted and cannot create anything new. The child is a sign of the need for a new beginning, so radically new that it shocks even the Christian who should know better. It would be a mistake to read Graham Greene's novel only as a vindication of traditional Christianity in its struggle with a new-fangled ideology committing all kinds of crimes in the most tyrannical manner. The struggle is not external—between Christianity and the world—but internal—within Christianity itself, against itself. Bernanos's priest can be put side by side with Greene's.

The corruption outside cannot be fought while there is corruption inside. First to be eradicated is the corruption within. Both novelists approach the problem of Christianity's position in today's culture from this angle. Greene's priest looks outside into the enemy—and sees there what he would find as a lack or as a tumor within Christianity. Bernanos's priest looks inside himself, but his sins and his failures are not only personal; they describe the paralysis of the Christian faith itself. By means of their analysis of the priest's predicament both Bernanos and Greene descend into the human struggle "to learn other things besides despair and love, that a man can be unwelcome even in his own home."

Here it is not the priests' fate that is of interest: Faith can be unwelcome even in Christianity; such Christianity is no better than rubbish. In *The Power and the Glory* there is a scene in which the whisky priest drops his case on a heap of rubbish: "a whole important and respected youth dropped among the cans—he had been given (this case) by his parishioners in Concepcion on the fifth anniversary of his ordination." The scene, drawn in the postwar Italian cinematographic school of realism, is followed by a confrontation between the (humanly and ecclesiastically) illegitimate father and his daughter. Immediately, he feels "aware of his own desperate inadequacy." His inadequacy is more than a sign of humility. It represents the fact that the kind of faith for which he stands in spite of the enemies without as well as within is on the verge of extinction. Inadequate, he might as well have ceased to live. "Where he was going it would be as if God in all this space between the sea and the mountains ceased to exist." The present is a time of transition. Things seem to remain unchanged and yet they pass—just as in the revolutionary Mexico of Graham Greene's novel still stand churches and buildings of a time now past. One can pass these churches by as if they are there, but in them there is no life: "They passed the whitewashed church—that too belonged to a dream. Life didn't contain churches." Greene's priest can, now that life does not contain churches, have faith because he no longer has any reasons to have faith. He can count on the grace of God not because his shortcomings make it even more necessary, but because they do not make it necessary at all. For him, all is grace because he has practically ceased to wear his clerical garb.

But those for whom life still contains churches continue to believe that religion consists in avoiding social changes, in protecting the family, in defending the *status quo,* in believing that life must be centered around the church no matter what the church is like. It is this kind of religion that Bernanos attacks in *The Diary of a Country Priest.* The sophisticated priest of this religion may be quite eloquent and a stanch defender of law and order; he may criticize the passion to change society for the sake of changing it; but he is at the same time the chief culprit of the secularization of Western culture. Bernanos was not mistaken. Though the world of his novels is darkness and light in such a way that the light makes darkness even darker, he realized that the most potent enemy of faith was not the secular mind as such but its creator, the sophisticated priest full of wind: "The priest who descends from the pulpit of Truth, with a mouth like a hen's vent, a little hot but pleased with himself; he's not been preaching: at best he's been purring like a tabby-cat."[3] Later, in the same novel, Bernanos says more explicitly: "What's wrong with the clergy?—Not much, except that they have secularized us." That is to say, they have alienated Christianity and Western culture from each other. "There is no longer," adds Bernanos, "there will no longer be any Christendom."

Contrast Bernanos's dialogue between the priest and a faithful named Arsène and the story of Caesarea Philippi in the New Testament. In the latter, Jesus asks his disciples what kind of rumor goes on about him. Then he adds: "And you, who do you say that I am?" Peter immediately answers, and his answer is well known: "Thou art the Christ, the Son of the living God." The confession of Peter, cornerstone of the whole faith of the Church, is concerned with life; it is centered on the meaning of life. It seems as if such a starting point must lead somewhere.

But the dialogue between the priest and Arsène takes another turn. "What do people think of me in the parish?" The first question is almost identical with that of Jesus. Similarly, the priest asks, too: "And you, what do you think of me, you, Arsène?"

No bursting confession follows upon this question. Arsène seems to hesitate, to look for an answer. His first words have nothing to do with the question. He talks about this or that, wonders what conversion means, he has never seen that phenomenon, but he and his family have all and always belonged to the church. They have all died properly, that is to say, after the last rites, although, Arsène adds, "When one is dead, everything is dead."

Jesus's question brings to Peter the vision of a

new life. The priest's question calls for an image of
death and decay. There is no remedy to death or
to decay—at least none that might be prescribed
by the clergy, by the church, by Christianity.
Western culture must look elsewhere if it wishes
to find an alternative to its corrosion. At the
hands of Christianity it will suffocate more and
more. The last rites are of no avail. Besides, they
tell you that you are really dead. There is no
remedy for death, for the death of the old order
presided over by Christianity and for the death
of all that the country priest attempted to transform.

Parallel with the agonizing attempts of the
priest, there lurks one sign of hope in the texture
of the novel. This hope stems from the personality
of a defrocked priest, an old friend of the country
priest. The reasons for his leaving the priesthood
are not clearly stated. They do not need to be expressed. But the effects of his new orientation are
unmistakably set forth. "You must have long since
realized," he says to the country priest, "that I
have, as they say left the habit [*quitté la soutane*].
My heart, though, has not changed. Only it is now
open to a conception of life *more human and consequently more generous*" (italics added).

Is there in these words a suggestion of a remedy
for the death of the old Christian culture of the
West? What the country priest is seeking is also
a more human and accordingly more abundant
conception of existence. He, too, can be considered
as a defrocked priest, spiritually if not ecclesiasti-

cally. There is between their modes of life a rap-
port which the boundary of the church cannot
obliterate. Whether within or without the church,
within or without that ossified community of men
called Christians, only one exit is available to
those who realize the agony of Christianity. It lies
in acknowledging the fact that Christianity has
ceased to inform life and, moreover, that under
the circumstances it cannot hope to be able ever
to do so again. What the dying country priest has
found and what caused the defrocked priest to
leave the church are one and the same thing. In
theological language, it is expressed in the final
words of the dying priest to his former colleague:
"All is grace." It is in the name of this grace that
the country priest has suffered and alienated himself from an ineffective Christianity. It is also in
the name of this same grace that his former com-
panion has left the physical community of Christianity.

"All is grace." These last words of the country
priest constitute a critique of Christianity rather
than of secularism. Bernanos criticizes Christianity
by reason of his faith in God's presence even in a
world torn by inhuman passions. But the fact is
that his novels almost universally describe a world
in which one thing is evident, and that is God's
absence. It is Christianity which is responsible for
God's absence from the structures of Western culture. It is no use recalling that this culture owes
its existence to Christianity. Today, the situation
has so changed that one must rebel against Chris-

(117)

tianity either if one wants to believe in God or if one wants to save Western culture from its progressive decay. The two priests of *The Diary* represent these two possibilities.

Here, then, is the significant dimension of religious novels similar to *The Diary* or *The Power and the Glory.* In the last decades there has been a resurgence of such novels. Almost always they portray as the central figure a priest whose actions take place in the context of a post-Christian era. The role of the priest is more prophetic than sacerdotal, just as it is more anticlerical than clerical. A parallelism with the priest-workers cannot fail to strike us. For the priest of the novel as well as for the priest-worker, the church is the stumbling-block. If it often represents law and order, it also represents the petrified past. It sets itself aside from or above the contemporary condition of man, economically and culturally.

In these so-called religious novels, it is not the church, as an institution, but the priest as an individual who is the protagonist. No wonder André Blanchet bitterly complained about the treatment accorded the church, as he remarked that the church no longer occupies the center of the stage if it appears at all. The Archbishop, who in Gilbert Cesbron's novel about the priest-workers typified the old clerical view of Christianity, says reprovingly: "We are no longer the primitive church: we are the Roman Catholic Church."[4] The priest-figure in this type of novel is quite remote from the classical priest who, consciously representing

the official church, acted as spiritual director or
omnicompetent manager. André Blanchet notes
this point in his book on the priest in the contemporary novel. It is surprising to see that he does
not realize his self-contradiction when, on the one
hand, he welcomes this change, and, on the other,
he concedes that the old-type priest often was an
obstacle, sealing off Christ from the faithful whose
life he directed. Father Blanchet dislikes Bernanos's priest because he does not in his estimation
adequately typify a normal diocesan priest, but
resembles a monk let loose in a village or a simple
layman touched by the Spirit. A Bernanos priest,
says Father Blanchet, is more like a layman—"all
that he does, a layman could do, too." Rather
unexpectedly Blanchet makes a distinction between a person who is God's *witness* and one who
is a *minister, i.e.* officer, of the church: he regrets
that the religious novel in general and Bernanos's
in particular prefer to deal with the witness rather
than with the officer of the church.

For André Blanchet, authentic existence cannot
be severed from the old cultural moorings of
which the church was the guardian. Bernanos, as
well as Greene and many others, is saying precisely
the opposite. When the country priest on his
deathbed hallows the life and the example of the
defrocked priest by insisting that "all is grace," he
is acknowledging that authentic existence no
longer depends upon one's membership in the
church or upon one's allegiance to Christianity.
Someone other than the defrocked priest (who

according to canon law still remains a priest) could have administered the last rites. But that would have been against the expressed will of the dying country priest.

In François Mauriac's *The Lamb*,[5] the protagonist is openly a former priest-to-be. Having changed the course of his life just as he is on his way to the seminary, he voluntarily gets involved in the conjugal difficulties of a young couple. He succeeds in helping them overcome their troubles and continues to live in their village, but not without coming under the unfriendly eye of the local priest. In the end, he dies in an accident which looks both like a murder and like a suicide. It is as if, having found authentic existence outside the church, he was prevented from living it to its fullest extent. He became alive only as he found a vocation outside the church, outside the pale of organized Christianity.

Would it be an exaggeration to say that even as this young man found his true self after he turned away from his initial vocation, so also Western culture is trying to find its own self in shaking off the crippling shackles of a superannuated Christianity?

Samuel Beckett's *Waiting for Godot* is an invitation to shake off the fetters that still link Western man to a past Christian culture. The whole play is constructed around the irrelevance of Christian concepts and especially around the nonsensical or quixotic quality of Christian existence. Such existence is based on the belief that there is a God who particularly cares for man and is ever loving and concerned enough to enter the scene of man's destiny. Two of the characters, Gogo and Didi, wait for him to do so. Somehow God never quite manifests himself. What remains of him in the fatigued imagination of those who wait for him is a caricature of his tamed majesty. That is why he is called Godot, the ending of that name having a diminutive connotation. Godot is a symbol of man's vacuous and errant imagination. Man clings in his mind to this symbol as if he could not do without it. In actuality he could live without it just as well. In the passage about a summer honeymoon on the shores of the Dead Sea, Gogo stresses the anachronism of Christian existence. Symbolically, nothing could more derisively and decisively convey the feeling that Christianity is indeed a dead alternative to man's contemporary predicament, a dead end to his quest for life. The texts that are bound between the covers of the Bible have no contemporary meaning whatever for Gogo, and presumably they have none for modern man.

Using a Christian theme and symbolism, Beckett points to a Christianity whose God has become for the Christians an emotional outlet and nothing more. Christians do not behave in relation to their God in any better way than do Gogo and Didi in relation to their Godot.

In Beckett's eyes, Christians have actually made their God into a Godot. If then, from a Biblical point of view, Beckett's Godot has all the attributes of an idol, Christians must now ask themselves whether or not they are guilty of idolatry. In point of fact, Gogo and Didi are the average Christian watching the play. But Beckett masterfully prevents him from effecting such a substitution: he forces him to face the irrelevance of Christianity.

Beckett successfully achieves this end by reversing the meaning of the Christian symbols. These symbols, by virtue of their sacramental nature, stress the necessity of cleansing natural man. With Beckett, they point to the urgency of cleansing culturally Christian man, with a view to bringing out natural man. As Thoreau, Whitman, and transcendentalism (*i.e.* Puritanism upside down) used the Bible with the intention of divesting Puritanism of any intrinsic worth, so Beckett uses Christianity in order to point out its anachronism. His dexterity has the sharp effectiveness of Sartre's laconic salutation in an address to newspapermen gathered in Geneva after the war: "Gentlemen, God is dead."

All Is Grace Because God Is Dead

The countereffect of Christian influence on Western man can be measured by going from *Waiting for Godot* to Archibald MacLeish's *J.B.* Godot, or the substitute god with whom Beckett seems even less satisfied than with the Christian God, is the real source of the modern Job's tragedy as conceived by MacLeish. Beckett, who does not

believe in God, believes even less in Godot. Mac-
Leish, on the contrary, seems to be saying that
Godot is all that there is of God. In Beckett's
play it is clearly intimated that Godot lives only
in man's imagination. But MacLeish constructs
his play around this secondhand God by inviting
us to thank man's imagination for allowing Godot
to come into existence. Beckett reveals and pleads
for everything that man has to gain from aban-
doning all atavistic attachment to a deity. His is a
thoroughgoing humanism, more like Camus's than
like Sartre's. But MacLeish's humanism is more
like Sartre's than like Camus's. With Sartre, Mac-
Leish declares that if God existed, man could
not bear not being that God. Beckett is thus
psychologizing God away, while MacLeish deifies man.

The distance between Biblical man and post-
Christian man can be shown by comparing Job
and J.B. Job's predicament is that, though he believes in God, he acts at times as if he doubted.
But he cannot be convinced by his doubt. At the
end, his tragedy comes to the point: Without God,
man would be nothing. J.B.'s predicament is that
he does not believe in God, but acts as if he does
or wishes he did. At the end of his tragic life he
clearly states that without man there would be
no God.

The first characteristic of wisdom literature is
its existential (the word is quite appropriate) concern about man and his destiny. But this concern
about the meaning of existence does not evolve

into a theory about history or about the future. Human existence is even viewed in such a way that this view gives the impression of being too simple. According to it, existence is authenticated by the antinomy between wisdom and folly. Furthermore, wisdom is a concomitant of piety; and piety—or *grace*—is another face of justice, whether human or divine. Therefore, wisdom is also a reflection of God's wisdom. There is, then, a strict correlation between man's wisdom and God's wisdom, man's justice and God's justice. If God is good, he is just, and his justice is neither blind nor a mere theologoumenon. That is, God's justice stands revealed in the wisdom and piety of man—in the pious, the *grace*ful life.

Wisdom literature shows a further dimension of its depth: human experience belies the correlation between man's wisdom and God's wisdom, between man's justice and God's justice: the just man suffers. What does this mean? For wisdom literature, God's justice is something more than retributive justice; and the wisdom of God is something other than the total of man's wisdom. This leads to a tragic view of life. But the tragic element has uncommon quality: its source is not to be found in the mystery of evil or the frustration of man's action but in the fact that both the justice and the injustice, the wisdom and the folly of man invariably point to the *otherness* of God despite, or precisely because of, the underlying correlation between God's and man's wisdom. Even in faith God remains wholly other

(1 2 4)

than man. One cannot therefore deduce God's existence from the amount of justice in the world, or deny it because of evil and human suffering. The tragic sense of life according to Biblical thought lies in the fact that suffering, that human experience as a whole, is what separates man from *himself.* Theologically speaking, the presence of God is a mystery or an abyss. From this angle human experience appears as the threat to existence, as the possibility of self-alienation. Above and beyond this threat, and redeeming man from it, there is the affirmation of God's faithfulness to man. Irrational as this view may seem, it follows another logic than that of logic—that of human experience. It is an analytic description of, not a theory about, human existence. Faith, therefore, is the response of the wise man's vision that all is grace. It cannot be justified by any theory of reward and punishment. Faith is not a justification of reasons, good or bad. Nor is God "reasons," as he is claimed to be in the beginning of MacLeish's *J.B.*

The Book of Job and *J.B.* represent two conceptions of man which are worlds apart. "God is just" becomes in today's secular version "God is reasons." He is the Cosmic Pal; he can be useful. J.B. says: "I've always known that God was with me"; he is "good to me." God is on J.B.'s side. He is just about all the good things that J.B. is. He is the spit and image of J.B. He is so many reasons that he does not really exist in the beginning of the play, just as J.B. himself exists only as a figment, or at best potentially, until his tragedies begin to unfold. It is only gradually that, as the problem of God's existence becomes more explicit, God seems to take on flesh.

The problem that *J.B.* proposes to solve, and does solve in its manner toward the end, is lodged in the compound proposition that God, if he is God, is not "good," and that if he is "good" he is not God. *J.B.* himself indicates the origin as well as the implication of this dilemmatic riddle by stating that man's innocence and the existence of God are mutually exclusive. This statement is echoed by Sarah's question and the affirmative answer it implies, when she asks whether God purchases his innocence at the expense of man's. Not without some existential reminiscences, the caustic Nickles too describes man's condition according to the current *Zeitgeist:* man's life is not of his own choosing, nor is his presumed guilt; with or without the euphemism of God's mercy, man is the lonely and innocent proprietor of his own "dirty self."

The thesis of *J.B.* seems *at first* to revolve around the following proposition: The meaning of existence is to justify God. Man is, therefore God is. "God is reasons," declares Zuss in the beginning of the play. At the end, when *J.B.* has received his "dirty self" back, he can say, "God is." As in Biblical thought, there is a correlation between man's wisdom and God's, between God and man. But now God depends upon man for his existence. And that is not all. If man is nothing except perhaps God's creator, his guilt is precisely that he has created God: God "is unthinkable if we are innocent." God is, but must be justified at the expense of man's misery. And man is the more miserable the more he tries to justify this God whom he has created.

Is there no alternative to this absurd existence? There is. For the play then modifies its thesis and insinuates this question: Why should man, like a Sisyphus, continually attempt to justify God, especially if all he seeks to accomplish is to find *his own raison d'être?* Could it not be that his predicament in justifying God is not really related to *his raison d'être?* Why try to prove God, if all that man needs is to be himself? Why seek God, if all that man wants is love? Anyway, is not this quest for God just a quest for love? Sarah expresses this point of view by saying that she could not help J.B. any more; that his God is a God of justice, but there is no justice. A just God has nothing to do with life. Existence is moved by another force, love—which God is lacking. For to J.B. God does not love, he only is.

In the Biblical perspective God is love because he *is.* A God who is and does not love and is not faithful to man might as well be dead. Though "he is," J.B.'s God, or rather, J.B.'s "Godot," is dead. But the man who seeks love must also seek justice, and therefore he creates God.

A strange paradox (if it is one) remains. Man needs to create for himself a God on whom he depends for all things. This God, if he exists, de-

pends on man for one thing even more important
than his being, since man cannot ascertain it—
God depends on man for love. This one thing can-
cels out all the others, especially those things for
which man depends on God or because of which
he conceives God. Does not man's capacity for
love ultimately cancel out God himself? As Sarah
says, there is neither justice nor divine love, there
is only human love. Job, in the Biblical myth,
could not understand suffering and evil because
for him God's existence was not in question. But
J.B., or post-Christian man, does not understand
evil and suffering because God does not really
exist except theoretically. For him, only love "is,"
and it is when it is freely given in spite of suffering, of injustice, of death, and, finally, of God. And
yet, in the face of God's uselessness, this love paradoxically justifies Godot, any Godot. To the viril-
ity of love succeeds a sheer sentimentality.

Actually, it is not the question of God or of
religious existence that preoccupies the contemporary mind, but a materialistic question of utility,
of success. For example, there is no giving of
thanks in J.B.'s family at the Thanksgiving dinner.
The dinner does not stress any God-centered
family life. J.B. does not consider his position and
his family affluence as a blessing from God. The
dinner simply demonstrates that all that wealth is
the product of J.B.'s craft and skill. He could not
be bothered by his spiritual mediocrity—he is not
even conscious of it.

The cult of reassurance and success is the promoter of the recent revival of religion. MacLeish is right in interpreting the predicament of a modern Job in terms of that cult.

Outside of the religiosity which hovers over *J.B.*, there is another aspect of the play which equally clearly situates it in a time withdrawn from the influence of Christianity. *J.B.* is a modern tragedy. Yet the tragic element itself is rather thin and insufficiently convincing, even if the events that disturb the middle-class tranquillity of *J.B.* are rather cataclysmic. But a succession of misfortunes is not a tragedy. Certainly, it is not there that one would seek the elements of a tragedy; one would seek it in the human attitude assumed by *J.B.* in the midst of his vicissitudes. This attitude is not quite correlated with the supposed tragic intensity of the events. The reason for this lack of correlation is not so much the superficiality of *J.B.*'s plight (which is, indeed, a little too technological) as the inescapable feeling that the adversities which fall upon him do not ultimately affect his self-understanding. It is not the events themselves that should contain the tragic element so much as *J.B.*'s self-understanding. No spectator would need the theatrical succession of sound and fury to realize that *J.B.*'s tragedy is a false tragedy.

Either no tragedy is possible today because the present age is neither Greek nor Christian; or, if *J.B.* or any other similar play is to be seen as a tragedy, then it is a new form of tragedy which bears no resemblance either to the Greek or to the Christian conception. In the Greek conception necessity determines the tragic course of human existence. Beyond the problem of necessity and freedom, or determinism and free will, the fatalistic character of the Greek tragedy results from the fundamental dualism underlying the Greek concept of life. Against this background the inescapable sequence of tragic events which falls upon an individual corresponds to the Greek attempt to express the unity of human existence. With or without the gods' favor, life is one.

In the Christian view, the concept of man's freedom adds a new dimension to the relationship between God and man. Therefore the Christian view is neither dualistic nor monistic, but it has an equal apprehension of the unity of human existence. The tragedy consists in that instead of this kind of life, one could lead that kind of life.[7]

Both the Greek and the Christian concepts are religious and supernaturalistic. They necessitate an absolute, or at least the existence of a principle other than the human. But supernatural beliefs have today lost their relevance. No attempt to find their equivalents inside the framework of a self-contained human existence will produce a satisfactory alternative either to the Greek or to the Christian conception of tragedy. As Camus realized, to posit the absurdity of life is not enough. It is not even a pure negation, and is, consequently, only a penultimate cry of despair before the ultimate affirmation of life. Suicide would be the only form of tragedy that could possibly have some plausibility. But before he committed suicide, man would have to deny it has any meaning. And the tragedy would lose its plausibility. In a golden age of religiosity there is less and less room for a tragic conception of life.

The disappearance of tragedy is further evident in the portrayal of a Christ-figure as the central character in so many contemporary novels. While the literary effects, even the religious ones, can be tremendous, the theological implication is disastrous.[8] The Christ-figure is a result of the process of leveling down. If all is grace, any man can take on the marks of Christ; and Christ, the unique, according to Christian theology, becomes a mere mask, suitable to any man. The Christ-figure is but another devaluation of Christianity. It is expressive of the broad secularization of Christian concepts, whose content has been hollowed out. The humanization of God—or the deification of man which takes place in many ideologies, from communism to some forms of existentialism—indeed goes hand in hand with the secularization of Christ and the assimilation of Christianity with a culture which *ipso facto* is less and less Christian.

There is a deeper level in the predicament of modern man, which *J.B.* reflects by dealing neither with the problem of being nor with that of suicide. There is no better proof than this lacuna that the illusion of an afterlife has no hold over modern man. The master of this world and constantly beset by imponderables, man may not feel a sense of deliverance from evil or from the oppression of non-being, but at least he feels bound to something, namely the possibility of circumventing the absurd. Modern man is neither awed by the death of God nor perplexed by the problem of suicide. He is represented neither by Nietzsche nor by Camus. For Nietzsche the death of God meant a feeling of deliverance; and for Camus it leaves man confronted with the only real philosophical problem, that of suicide. Either way, both express their thought in the terms of a cultural approach to man's self-understanding which, though peripherally, still is influenced by Christianity. The death of God supposedly liberated man from the problem of understanding himself in terms of a transcendental allegiance to a supernatural power unable to justify the evil of this world. From probing the problem of suicide, there may emerge an affirmation of life or the necessity of self-transcendence as the essence of life. This still poses the problem of man in the framework of transcendence, even though the latter is now neither supernaturalistic nor futuristic. Transcendence in Nietzsche and Camus only indicates a desperate effort to overcome despair. Love, however, finite and concrete love, is more adequate and apt to overcome despair. Not that love can *finally* become the condition of existence, but that it may do so *once again*, as Camus would say, or only once more.

J.B. is neither Sisyphus nor one of Dostoevski's characters tormented about the death of God. The idea of suicide never arises on his destitute horizon. Nor does he ever think of usurping God's place, since for him there is no transcendental God. In spite of the thunder and the catastrophes, J.B. is more like Gide's Nathanael than like Sisyphus or Ivan Karamazov or Kirilov. It is less problematic to assert life and to go on living when man is confronted with God's silence, as J.B. advocates (and one can always find a substitute), than it is when man is confronted with the silence of this world (for which there is no substitute). More like Don Juan than like anyone else, J.B. conquers and wastes. He is neither committed to others nor a derelict and alienated from others. For him existence is not a tragedy; he denies that it should be. This may be the greatest illusion to replace the Christian vision of life. Illusion or not, it has succeeded to the illusion of an afterlife.

The religiosity manifested in *J.B.* is narcissistic. Though it deals with a god which is nothing other than love itself, this god, or this love, is a purely human phenomenon. It is not an absolute above and beyond man. It does not confront man with a transcendental reality wholly other than himself. Sinfulness, or anxiety before that which threatens man from the outside, is totally absent from J.B.'s moral struggle. In theological words, he does not stand before God. He does not have to choose between a relative and the absolute, between the transitory and the permanent, between God and "reasons." In *J.B.*, man may no longer afford the luxury of thinking himself the measure of all things; he may even turn his back on the sentimental and immanental theism of the nineteenth century, centered on the cult of God's fatherhood and the brotherhood of men. A certain god may have become the measure of J.B.'s existence, his affections and his struggles and his predicament; but it is a god who reflects the image of man all too faithfully. Besides, what else could this god be, since the contemporary framework of man's self-understanding is, as *J.B.* shows, no longer transcendental?

PART TWO

THE
CULTURAL AGONY
OF
CHRISTIANITY

CHAPTER VII

Cultural Incapacity for God: The Absence of God's Reality

THEOLOGICALLY speaking, every age is post-Christian. This means that every man and every situation stand under God's judgment. They constantly need to be measured against the yardstick of God's justice and must be, time and again, redeemed from their natural propensity toward corruption and sinfulness. Just as no man is holy once and for all, so also no situation exhibits the reality of God's presence once and for all. If men are in need of constant renewal, human achievements and cultural realizations need to be revised almost instantaneously. This applies to every man, to every generation, to every age. It applies particularly to Christendom and even more particularly to Christianity, especially at a time when the churches have comfortably slipped into the hedonism of religiosity.

Such a claim about the post-Christian character emerges directly from the New Testament. Quite apart from the Book of Revelation—really the first book to claim that "this age" is post-Christian —Jesus on more than one occasion during his lifetime rebuked his disciples for lacking faith, although they were full of religiosity, as Peter was when he thought that the Christ could not suffer. Jesus even observed: "When the Son of Man comes, will he find faith on earth?"

The Christian ideals of one generation invariably degenerate by the time another generation rises up. But Christendom in the past always displayed enough strength to correct this process. The parallelism between the situation of the last century and a half and that of Christendom's expansion into the barbarian provinces of Europe is pertinent. Charles Williams's assessment of the Christianization of those areas fits the predicament of modern Christianity:

The missionaries pressed out with the Gospel precisely as the parish priests baptized babies. Christendom moved outward in space as it attempted to move forward in time. There is no other institution which suffers from time so much as religion. At the moment when it is remotely possible that a whole generation might have learned something both of theory and practice, the learners and their learning are removed by death, and the Church is confronted by the necessity of beginning all over again. The whole labour of regenerating mankind has to begin again every thirty years or so.[1]

Charles Williams goes on to indicate the reason why the present situation differs from that of Christendom in the Dark Ages. The difference is that "in spite of all its temptations and difficulties Christendom had really achieved a nature." It is this "nature" which is now spent or does not accord itself with the modern condition of man.

Because this age is post-Christian *culturally*, Christianity has lost its relevance. Being intrinsically bound to a decaying cultural pattern, it cannot extricate itself from the compromises it has engendered and the allegiances by which it shaped the past. To say, therefore, that this age is post-Christian culturally is a much more serious indictment of Christianity than the homiletic reminder that every age comes anew under God's judgment. The latter is meaningful only to the extent that Christianity really and positively acts as a leaven in any given cultural framework. But, today, the structures of the world have changed from top to bottom and Christianity, it seems, has been left out of them.

Retrospect and Prospect

This age is post-Christian not only *theologically* but also *culturally*. *Theologically*, no age, no culture, no nation, no society, is Christian, just as no man *is* but *becomes* a Christian, continually. This age is post-Christian culturally in that man cannot even *become* a Christian. The fundamentals of our culture—those things that govern our self-understanding—make us impervious to the conception of Christianity.

The world-view of Christianity is transcendental, ours is immanental; the divergence is not only theological, it is also cultural. The leveling down can be seen not only in the failure of faith and the quest for consistency which accompany it; it can also be seen in the social and political realms. Western culture has evinced the masks of this leveling down; since the end of the eighteenth century, almost every historical event points to it.

Both the American and the French Revolutions not only brought social and political changes; they also ushered in, or simply endorsed, cultural as well as theological transformations. Political liberty was and remains the most spectacular achievement of these two revolutions. But the American Revolution was also the herald of theological liberty, as shown by the subsequent First Amendment of the American Constitution. The French proclaimed the same ideal by more or less official attempts to mark the end of what might be called the ecclesiastical era of Western culture. On the American Continent, the traditional Christian concepts of ransom, redemption, and forgiveness were deprived of their ethical and social connotations and implications, and were taken over by the more democratic if not yet purely secular ideals of justice, constitutional government, and moral law.[2] Gradually, theological liberty, which at first meant freedom from dogmatic restraint or constraint, more and more imperturbably signified freedom from theology. Nor did it take long to find that concrete justice is a more relevant factor in the business of daily existence than any agreement or disagreement on a substitutionary theory about an otherworldly justice.

The French Revolution marks even more emphatically, though sometimes in a tragically ostentatious way, the repudiation of ecclesiastical authority and its exclusion from the pursuit of political emancipation and social adjustments. The decapitation of the French king not only is synonymous, as Camus suggests, with the death of God which Nietzsche was later to proclaim; it also brings to an end the ecclesiastically controlled civilization which Christianity had inspired until then. The Reformation had shaken this ecclesiastical control; but, in its beginnings at least, it had substituted the conception of a civilization reinforced by the sporadic control of various brands of theologies. In such matters the civilization built on the foundations of the Reformation was not less authoritarian, as Troeltsch points out in *Protestantism and Progress*, than the coercion exerted by Christianity in the Middle Ages. But by the beginning of the nineteenth century, both versions of Christian culture, one under ecclesiastic and the other under theological control, had officially been discarded. The ensuing expansion of Christianity in Africa and elsewhere was a posthumous tribute to the cultural significance of Christianity now superseded in its homeland.

Within the provinces of Christianity a secularization of religion had meanwhile been taking place, and the secular institutions now arrogated to themselves what sacral aura they could capture from the religious ones. The Rights of Man disestablished God's redemptive covenant, democracy evicted the communion of saints, and the attributes of God were now conceived as simply the highest predicates of man; but the divine and transcendental categories through which the purpose of human existence was annotated and elucidated did not expire. At the same time as God was identified with the essence of man, man himself was deified, and a general apotheosis enveloped and transfigured man no less than the tools and institutions with which he annexed the world and conquered his destiny.

In this context Ludwig Feuerbach, by the middle of the nineteenth century, could claim that "theology is anthropology"; that nothing other than the knowledge of man is divine; and that God is but a notion derived from the highest and purest predicates of man. All this Feuerbach candidly deduces from what he considers the essence of Christianity. Those that would accuse him of committing a sacrilege he rebuffs with the expostulation that when Christianity lowered God into man, it made man into God. Feuerbach was recording the collapse of theology, just as the French Revolution had recorded the disintegration of ecclesiastical dominion over civilization as well as the eclipse of God—which became a fact as soon as

God was conceived of as a clockmaker or an absentee landlord. The contemporary theologian Karl Barth argues in his essay on Feuerbach, that theology had already became anthropology, "Ever since Protestantism itself, and especially Luther, emphatically shifted the interest from what God is in himself to what God is for man. Its course of development runs uninterruptedly in such a direction that man more and more renounces God and addresses himself." In Feuerbach's words: "So long as man adores a good being as his God, so long does he contemplate in God the goodness of his own nature. . . . He who makes God act humanly, declares human activity to be divine; he says: A god who is not active, and not morally or humanly active, is no god; and thus he makes the idea of the Godhead dependent on the idea of activity, that is, of human activity, for a higher he knows not."[3]

The classical dogmas have lost one of their chief functions, that of protecting man's mind by delineating the sphere of human speculation and action, even as the City of God, under the aspect of the church, no longer delimits the area of social and political activity. In neither respect can Christianity pragmatically reinforce its claim as the protector of man's body or of man's mind. To neither field does it seem to be now pertinent. Retrospectively, this accounts for the ambiguous feeling discernible in Montesquieu's ejaculation: "*Chose admirable! La religion chrétienne, qui ne semble avoir d'objet que la félicité de l'autre vie, fait encore notre bonheur dans celle-ci"* ("Admirable thing! The Christian religion, which seems to have no purpose other than felicity in the afterlife, still makes our happiness in this life").[4] The advantages which the establishment of Christianity had allegedly procured for the human race, and which Turgot extolled in a discourse at the Sorbonne in 1750, were no longer self-evident; excepting that, for want of a more direct suzerainty of the Christian faith and morality over the ways of this world, the idea of an afterlife was still honored with some degree of acquiescence.

Cultural Incapacity for God

The post-Christian cultural framework in which modern man lives and moves is reflected in the contrast between the Christian and the modern conception of man. According to the former, human nature is understood within a transcendental frame of reference. Saint Paul said in the Areopagus, reminiscing a line from Epimenides for apologetic purposes: "In Him we live and move and have our being" (Acts 17:28). Whatever Epimenides meant, Saint Paul's point is that man knows himself in proportion as he knows God, and that he finds himself only if he seeks God. Saint Augustine later emphatically declared: *"Deum et animam scire cupio. Nihilne plus? Nihil omnino"* (God and the soul do I desire to know. Nothing more? Nothing at all). In the sixteenth century, Calvin was even more systematically emphatic when he began the first paragraph of his major work, the *Institutes of the Christian Religion*, with these statements:

> True and substantial wisdom principally consists of two parts, the knowledge of God and the knowledge of ourselves. But, while these two branches of knowledge are so intimately connected, which of them precedes and produces the other, is not easy to discover. For in the first place, no man can take a survey of himself but he must immediately turn to the contemplation of God. . . . Nor can we really aspire toward him, till we have begun to be displeased with ourselves. . . . On the other hand, it is plain that no man can arrive at the true knowledge of himself, without having first contemplated the divine character, and then descended to the consideration of his own.[5]

Even the interpretation of the essence of Christianity in Harnack's liberal theology has two foci: "God and the soul; the soul and its God."

No doubt contemporary theologians would agree on the interdependence of the knowledge of God and self-knowledge. But they do so in a different context. This context is non-Christian in a more basic sense than Bishop Lilje depicted it when he declared: "The scenery for Christianity has changed in our time more deeply and more fundamentally than most church people realize. We do live, for all practical purposes, in a non-Christian world."[6] If only the scenery were non-Christian, the contrast between now and past epochs of Christianity would be simply one of degree; but the difference is so fundamental that it can only be depicted by pointing to the *culturally* post-Christian nature of this age.

This period is not even anti-Christian. If it were non-Christian or anti-Christian, one could be witness unto it, even a marytr. Any of these possibilities would appear natural. Holden Caulfield, in Salinger's *Catcher in the Rye,* reflects the true temper of the age when he remarks about ministers that "they all have these Holy Joe voices when they start giving their sermons. God, I hate that. I don't see why the hell they can't talk in their natural voice." There is no correlation any longer between the Christian faith and the modern situation of man. That is why Christianity seems, in the word of a post-Christian, "unnatural."

What is taking place on the stage of Western culture is not "a struggle against God for God," to use Jaspers's phrase in describing the Book of Job. In order to struggle against God for God, man needs faith. Such a struggle ceases as soon as faith dies. This faith has died from its own application. If the knowledge of God is essential to self-knowledge, the traditional Christian optimism about human destiny must be relevant to the human situation. That the Christian tradition realized this is shown historically by the philosophical, artistic, and even technological reality of Christian culture. The Christian tradition understood this relevance so well that it always affirmed in one form or another, though perhaps more or less unhappily, that commitment to God implied involvement in the world and, conversely, that man's involvement in the world should be concerned with the ultimate goal of God's glorification. Man's involvement in the affairs of this world was never separated from the transcendental frame of reference in which self-understanding took place.

Today only the reality of the world, in all its immediacy and its immanence, provides man with a context for possible self-understanding. This self-understanding is amputated from any necessity of a fundamental knowledge of God. It is easier to understand oneself without God than with God. Modern man lives in a world of immanence. If he is the prey of anxiety, it is not because he feels guilty before a just God. Nor is it because he fails to explain the justice and love of God in the obvious presence of evil and injustice. God is no longer responsible for the world —since he is dead. But man is. He cannot avoid assuming full responsibility for a world of immanence, in terms of which he knows and understands himself or seeks to do so. The dilemma of Christianity is that it taught man how to be responsible for his actions in this world, and for this world itself. Now man has declared God not responsible and not relevant to human self-knowledge. The existence of God, no longer questioned, has become useless to man's predicament and its resolution.

Jean Giono's position is logical: Only a human

paganism can save modern man, or a deliberately post-Christian humanism like that of Camus and many others. In contrast to the Christian position which advocates, "Find God and you will find yourself," this kind of humanism proposes, as a contributor to *The Village Voice* sums it up, "Find yourself and you will not need to find God." In the words of the Dean of the Harvard Divinity school: "[The post-Christian man] is not hostile to religion, or even concerned. He simply does not raise the religious question at all, not even in church."[7] The churches themselves continue to think that Christianity remains a positive factor in the shaping of the emergent civilization. So also did the Hellenistic syncretism of the dying Roman Empire believe concerning its religions.

Admittedly, not only was there no room for primitive Christianity within the structures of the Roman society, but its very nature excluded it from them. Yet it overcame them. Christopher Dawson, believing that contemporary Christianity is in a similar situation, writes with confidence: "The same tradition [which proved victorious over the pagan world in the past] exists today, for though the Church no longer inspires and dominates the external culture of the modern world, it still remains the guardian of all the riches of its own inner life and is the bearer of a sacred tradition." He goes on to interpret rather devoutly the contemporary invalidation of Christianity as a latent "movement toward Christian culture" and as a "return to our own fatherland—to the sacred tradition of the Christian past which flows underneath the streets and cinemas and skyscrapers of the new Babylon as the tradition of the patriarchs and prophets flowed beneath the palaces and amphitheaters of Imperial Rome."[8]

There are two major differences which Mr. Dawson eloquently overlooks. The first is that this civilization of asphalt and glamor and reinforced concrete is not merely pagan, it is primarily post-Christian; it is the heir of a Christian culture and its "sacred tradition." Secondly, primitive Christianity was, comparatively speaking, in a position of strength. It could afford to look forward, whereas twentieth century Christianity seems caught in a nostalgic whirl, and it looks backward to what is taken for a golden age. How could Christianity dissociate itself from the implications of its own cultural and technological achievements? Is it because Dawson and Maritain and Bonhoeffer think it could or should that they envision the flowering of a new Christian culture as a concrete possibility? How can they forget that all interplay of religion and culture creates bondage, and that religion is only significant to the degree that it is bound to a culture? Of course, the eventuality of commencing another interplay is plausible theoretically. But this plausibility hinges on the degree of receptivity the cardinal Christian categories will find in the structures of a given culture. How can this happen if these structures *have become* impervious to these categories?

The devaluation of the fundamental categories of the Christian faith, of those that gave birth to the Christian culture, has reached such a point that the imperviousness of our world to the ideas and values characteristic of Christianity can be observed in practice.

Medieval civilization spent itself on building churches, cathedrals, and monasteries. Today in Paris the tourist will visit Notre Dame, but he will also ride in the elevator to the top of the Eiffel Tower; or in New York, he will be attracted by the Empire State Building, or Radio City Music Hall, or Rockefeller Center at the same time as some imitation Gothic churches incongruously recreate for him a feeling of the past. Professor Sorokin claims that in the twelfth and thirteenth centuries 97 per cent of the subjects in the fine arts were devoted to religious motifs, against 3 per cent depicting secular life; and that, in the twentieth century, the ratio is almost exactly the opposite. Whatever else these figures may mean, they certainly indicate that the concern has shifted from transcendentals to immanentals.

The gap between the categories of the Christian faith and the realities and aspiration of this world grows wider and wider. This disparateness, becoming more and more accentuated, can only result in the withdrawal of this world from the trusteeship of Christianity. A question arises that cannot be silenced by mere assent to the Christian tradition—a twofold question dealing with the permanency of the Christian religion, and the fate

of Western culture. The question is this: Does
the present age manifest any need for categories
of faith? Or is the present stage of Western culture strongly enough mature and integrated to go
it alone—after having thanked Christianity for the
formative role it has played and forthwith dis-
missing it?

Christianity and the Present Cultural Crisis

Some Christians believe in the permanency of
the Christian religion and its cultural tradition.
Others, like Karl Jaspers, place on record their
radical pessimism about a culture which has become impervious to categories of faith.[9] They
argue that, unless this particular age is motivated
by some transcendental persuasion, its body and
soul will become paralyzed and total disintegration will both engulf this civilization and destroy
any grain of faith that might still be dormant in
it.

Still others are not so pessimistic either about
the imprudent present or the no less imprudent
future, which they think, will yield a new *raison
d'être.* Pitirim Sorokin has taken notice of, and set
into evidence, the transition from a sacral to a
secular form of culture: but he vehemently dis-
agrees with those who claim that in the present
crisis Western culture and society are agonizing
to their death. His argument seeks to invalidate
the theories based on a biological analogy, that
"every culture and society should pass through

the stages of childhood, maturity, senility, and death." Claiming that no evidence for such a theory is irrefutably given, Sorokin argues in *The Crisis of Our Age* that "the complete disintegration of our culture and society . . . is impossible, also, for the reason that the *total sum* of social and cultural phenomena of Western society and culture has never been integrated into one unified system. What has not been integrated cannot, it is evident, disintegrate."[10] He does admit that the present crisis may signify "one of the greatest possible revolutions of our cultural and social life." By this Sorokin certainly cannot mean a comparatively simple change from one political or economic structure to another. He must mean the substitution of a fundamental idea of culture for another.

From any approach to the present crisis, the impact of Christianity on Western culture is no longer what it used to be. Is there yet any possibility of separating the denouement of the present desuetude of Christianity from that of today's crisis? So far as this age is post-Christian *culturally*, to what extent is the desuetude of Christianity a phenomenon only marking, or attributable to, the crisis this cultural system of values is undergoing and which Christianity, restored and rehabilitated, would ultimately outlast? A good tree needs pruning. Could it be that the current eclipse of Christianity is caused by an inevitable accumulation of cultural accessories that will in due time be cast away, especially since the more frequent and unmasking confrontations between Christians and non-Christian cultures will lay bare the decadent aspect of those accessories? Hypothetically, Christianity could then achieve a seminal and spiritual recovery which would set it on a new course.

Such a thesis rests on three assumptions. First, the fate of Christianity is not irrevocably but only partially bound to that of Western culture. Second, if such is the case, the crisis of this age is only a theological one. Third, the presumed vitality as well as the universality of the Christian religion is independent of the seeming disintegration of its cultural accomplishments. This threefold thesis does not deny the bond between Christianity and Western culture. It cannot therefore deny that Christianity is to some extent responsible for the decadence of Western culture. It concedes that the present crisis, because it is mainly cultural, is at the same time a religious, though not necessarily Christian, crisis. Accordingly, the conflict is not between Christianity and the contemporary cultural structures and values; it is between Christianity and antithetical values or anthropological systems, which are essentially religious although not Christian. In line with this general formulation, the conflict of religious forces becomes as a nodal agony within Christianity.

A similar crisis took place when Christianity, from being a Jewish sect, became the religion of all Europe, even while, diverging more and more radically from Judaism, it became the inheritor of the Greco-Roman legacy. In order to assert its universality Christianity had to discard a certain number of Jewish elements which were particularly restrictive or exclusivistic. On this theory, the present crisis is brought about by a threat to the validity and universality of Christianity by elements which subjugate it to a Western image of man and his place in the world. Shedding these elements, Christianity could once again emerge triumphant. Meanwhile its agony is understandable because it is critically difficult to disincarnate Christianity from the culture it has shaped and on which it depends. Can Christianity disentangle itself from concepts which are now regarded as exclusively Western, without ceasing at the same time to be Christian? Did not early Christianity almost irreparably undergo a radical change when it broke away from Judaism in order to settle down in the European nations? In the same way that Christianity then seemed to stand or fall with its essential bond of kinship with Judaism, Christianity today seems to stand or fall with Western culture.

In *Civilization on Trial*, Arnold Toynbee contends that "in contrast to the cyclic movement of the rises and falls of civilizations the history of religion on earth is a movement in a single continuous upward line."[11] By extension, this would mean that if the religious sentiment, under one shape or another, has been progressing in an upward line, it will not necessarily preserve its Christian shape. Religion may be here to stay. This does not imply that Christianity is. Religiosity is as different from Christianity as the movement of religion is, according to Toynbee, from that of culture. That religiosity will not disappear simply because Christianity is ebbing is clear enough from evidences as disparate as the Soviet ideology, the burgeoning Buddhist Mission to Germany, the attraction of Zen Buddhism, and the literature of the Beat Generation.

Apparently Toynbee does not consider the question from that angle. He intimates that what might take place is a grafting of religious elements, especially of the Far East, on to Christianity in the same way, he contends, as Christianity during the Roman Empire adopted the best of the other Oriental religions. When Rome fell, Christianity was its heir. Likewise, when the decline of this civilization has been completed and Christianity has profited by its confrontation with the other higher religions, Christianity may be left as their spiritual as well as cultural heir.[12] Meanwhile, the primordial task is to purge Christianity of its Western accretions and to liberate it from its Western exclusivism. Toynbee is not here saying that Christianity is the best religion; but he does say that it may become the best religion, especially since religion progresses in an upward direction. He is not assigning any uncontestable superiority to Christianity or perpetuating the myth of Christianity's hegemony—at least not in the way this has until recently been done. But he is certainly implying that the future of Christianity does not hang on the doom of Western culture, and that all the higher religions can culminate in an expurgated and reinvigorated type of Christianity, presumably because there is within Christianity a latent tendency toward universality.

A certain number of fallacies or misconceptions taint this argument and the assumptions it is based on.

First of all, there is some validity in the claim that Christianity is not bound up with Western culture. It did not sufficiently penetrate the civilization it inherited from Greece and Rome—and it is not apt to do so now or in the future. There has been, as it were, a complicity between Christianity and what became Western culture. They have been conspirators and now the masks are falling. Martin Buber points out that what was or is called Christendom differed significantly from the various nations that constituted it. As the continuous struggle between the papacy and the various monarchs indicates, the consciousness of the Church was superimposed over that of the different nationalities.[13] In so far as the first was not as strong as the second (since national loyalties never quite succumbed to the wider spiritual and cultural unity sought by the Church), the resulting unity of Christendom was less organic than the regional or national communities often were. The unification of moral and spiritual values was more desired than achieved: Western culture is precisely what supplies this unification. Paradoxically, it is not Christian enough for Christianity

(156)

to be bound up with it; but it is too Christian for Christianity to disown it at this critical juncture.

No matter how poorly the rest of his argument is carried on, this is what Dawson means in *The Historic Reality of Christian Culture* when he declares: "It is hardly too much to say that it is Christian culture that has created Western man and the Western way of life. But at the same time we must admit that Western man has not been faithful to this Christian tradition."[14] (Dawson can allow himself to argue that Christian culture has still a chance of winning the Western way of life. But inasmuch as he must uphold a certain degree of consanguinity between Christianity and Western culture, he may not both have his cake and eat it, too. He cannot attempt in good conscience to disculpate Christianity from the failure of Western culture. For, if "the revival of Christian civilization does not involve the creation of a totally new civilization, but rather the cultural reawakening or reactivation of the Christian minority,"[15] then it follows that whether their past relationship was successful or not, Christianity is bound up with Western culture.)

It is a truism to remark that "the revival of Christian civilization does not involve the creation of a totally new civilization." The problem does not deal with what a revival of Christian civilization would involve, so much as with the opportunity of such a revival. T. S. Eliot holds that this opportunity, in the last resort, may not be available to Christianity. In *The Idea of a Christian*

Society he states his belief that "the choice before us is between the formation of a new Christian culture, and the acceptance of a pagan one. Both involve radical changes; but I believe that the majority of us, if we could be faced immediately with all the changes which will only be accomplished in several generations, would prefer Christianity."[16] Perhaps. But the choice itself is not so clear cut. Eliot knows that in reality the crux of the matter is that the choice between a Christian and a post-Christian culture is not immediate—or, at least, it is consistent with itself in not *seeming* immediate. Even if, as Dawson claims, it is ultimately "a choice between Christianity or nothing," it does not follow from our present diagnosis of a choice not immediately before us that in Eliot's words "the only hopeful course for a society which would thrive and continue its creative activity in the arts of civilization, is to become Christian."[17] This amounts to saying that, except from a strictly homiletic standpoint, if Western culture falls, Christianity falls with it.

The fraud that authors like Eliot or Dawson commit is to think, as Troeltsch once put it, that Christianity is the loftiest and most spiritual revelation we know, and that it has the highest validity. In a lecture given at Oxford in 1923 on "The Place of Christianity Among the World Religions," Troeltsch repudiated this thesis, which he had once upheld.[18] He gave two types of reasons for his rejection of the thesis that Christianity's validity is supremely higher than that of the other religions.

The first are the scientifically or historically observable reasons from which he concluded that, regardless of the forms assumed by a religion, it cannot exist or manifest any validity without depending on a set of intellectual, social, and national conditions. From this, Troeltsch infers that the so-called supreme validity of a religion actually proceeds from a preferential treatment accorded the religio-cultural context into which a person is born. He concedes that, *mutatis mutandis,* all religions make similar claim. Their criterion for supreme validity operates only in the measure in which it has become ingrained in the texture of personal, social, or cultural conventions. Thus a religion has supreme validity only for those who have shaped and been shaped by it, who have begotten it and are nourished by it.

Lamennais indirectly anticipated this judgment. Attempting to base the authenticity and the supreme relevance of Christianity on an objective evidence, he starts from the premise that "certitude" is what the human race universally consents to. On this criterion, the reality and truth of the religious insight or aspiration are then developed, ultimately emerging into Christianity as into the apex of religion. Of course, this system would not have been hatched had not Lamennais been a victim of his particular religious sensitivity and had he not assented to a belief in the universal mission of Western culture.

From this analysis not only does the concept of the supreme validity of Christianity recede into the background, but the corollary claim of the universality of Christianity also loses its foundation.

The second kind of reasons concerns the view that the best of all the other higher religions can be assumed into Christianity. That, too, according to Troeltsch, is a fraud. It supposes that there is a common ground between Christianity and the other religions; then Christianity is declared either superior to them or the culmination of them. This kind of speculation only aims to retain the lost hegemony of Christianity. Its basic sophistry consists in equating universality or superiority with relevancy. Personal conviction may be quite justified in wishing such an equation. But in terms of objective facts and considerations it is difficult to find any instance confirming so personal a conviction beyond the limits of subjectivism. Troeltsch, easily realizing this, went a step further and "submitted that the mere fact of the universality of Christianity—of its presence in all the other religions—would, even if true—be irrelevant."

Troeltsch's insight could have been even deeper: not only is such an understanding of the universality of Christianity irrelevant historically or objectively (because it has yet to be proved in the actual confrontation, which always "takes several generations," and even corrodes the elements thus confronted); but also, were it to become a fact, such a universality would be vacuous from the Christian view itself. Neither its validity nor its universality is ultimate if it is not instinctive and immediate, just as humility ceases to be authentic if it is contrived and prompted by ulterior motives. How could Christianity become universal, and what could such universality mean, when Western man himself can hardly be said to be faithful to the Christian tradition, when the discrepancy between it and our culture is growing wider and wider? Christianity ceases to be universal not when it fails to supersede other religions or destroy other cultural traditions or cannot assume them; it ceases to be universal when, no longer relevant to its particular culture, it espouses foreign religio-cultural complexions. The relevance depends neither on the universality nor the supremacy of Christianity. It is comparatively easier to achieve a monopoly of universality or supremacy than to fecundate a culture which will incarnate the relevance. Neither mass baptisms nor the Crusades were an index of the relevance of Christianity. Gaining the world, Christianity would not necessarily preserve its soul.

Culture is as relevant to religion as the earth was to Adam's sweat. It is also a cage, just as

> The city is a cage.
> No other places, always this
> Your earthly landfall, and no ship exists
> To take you from yourself. Ah! don't you see
> Just as you've ruined your life in this
> One plot of ground you've ruined its worth
> Everywhere now—over the whole earth?[19]

Having squandered its responsibilities at home, Christianity can hardly claim to exercise them elsewhere or to be more authentic than any other religion. There is a sophisticated way of putting this: Christianity should not seek to impose itself. Maritain remarks that it is unbearably embarrassing to be confronted with the religious zeal of Mr. So-and-So, and to subject another person to one's own. Perhaps this is why he thinks that religious pluralism is now the only course of relevant Christian action, whether at home or abroad, within the fragmentation of Christian allegiance as well as in relation to non-Christian loyalties. Jaspers may well lament this growing impotence of the churches and the inefficacy of any humanism even distantly allied with the Christian tradition. It is a fact that Christianity no longer is the object of an absolute confidence.

The cleavage between Christianity and Western culture is an effect of the Christian tradition itself. This cleavage has a paradoxical accompaniment, in that Western culture is too Christian for Christianity to be dissociated from it. It is not Christian enough for its fate to be sealed with that of Christianity. It is evolving in a direction opposite from that of Christianity. To say that Christianity stands or falls with Western culture means that it stands or falls with the Christian elements of this culture. But these elements *have* fallen: this is the real meaning of the now religious, now immanentist, secularism typical of our age. The crisis of our age is involved with the substitution of secular for the Christian fundamentals of Western culture.

(162)

CHAPTER VIII

Cultural Disavowal of God: The Reality of God's Absence

THE problem of authority is perennial, but the dissolution of authority is one of the main characteristics of this post-Christian age. Evidenced today not only by religious syncretism or theological relativism, this dissolution is an effect of the scientific humanism which is replacing the Christian tradition as well as of a fatal misconduct on the part of Christianity. The crisis of authority is another aspect of the leveling down which has taken place in Western culture. This crisis is relevant to our thesis because authority is a symbol of faith. Even when, at its worst, it becomes an objectivation of faith, it still intends not to compel but to impel men's allegiance to a common ideal or belief. It is the objective expression of an ultimate concern, whereby the individual proposes to unmask and counteract the aggrandizement to apotheosis of his other concerns. In doing so, the individual acknowledges the impossibility of unifying objective reality and subjective truth.

Religious authority does not entail the eradication of personal autonomy for the sake of blind assent to a system of beliefs claiming the sanction of absolute or divine authority. But religious authority—when it is not superstitiously construed as an external power endowed with the wisdom of presenting a unified and coherent view of life and the world—symbolizes a synthesis of subjective truth and objective reality. This does not mean a *tertium quid* resting on their objectivized identification or their abstract unification. Through the symbol of authority, the individual disclaims absolute validity for his personal conviction, just as he refuses to surrender it to any external entity.

If a failure of faith provokes a squandering of authority or its usurpation, too much authority does not necessarily signify a greater demonstration of faith. On the contrary. Too much authority means not only *hybris*, or self-aggrandizement; it also means a violation of the structures of faith and their usurpation. It threatens the equilibrium between subject and object, between faith and reality. It does not destroy but sublimates the former. What this age is suffering from *primarily* is not a crisis of authority but a crisis of faith. Not that faith has slackened—it has been inflated. An inflationary faith typifies the crisis of this age.

(164)

Faith is an attempt to reconcile subject and object, subjective truth and objective reality, the self and the world, without overwhelming either one of the terms. Faith is an attempt to reconcile the two dimensions of existence—personal and impersonal, internal and external—without unifying them. It attempts to define man in terms of a synthesis or as the locus of a polarity and a tension between the absolute and the relative, the universal and the particular, the world and the self. It means that man does not live by logical consistency. Authority is a symbol of the kind of self-understanding man reaches through faith. By contrast, what characterizes our so-called religious as well as irreligious contemporaries is their common quest for logical consistency. That constitutes today the most vital opposition to the Christian tradition, and it comes from science and humanism, although both were formerly grounded in the Christian tradition.

The Christian Basis of Science and Humanism

From a strictly Christian point of view the supposed antagonism between religion and science is a false one. And in keeping with the classic fundamentals of the Western tradition, there cannot be any real antagonism between religion and science, between the province of religious authority properly conceived and the province of scientific investigation. Religious zealots who distrust science show that they do not understand the nature of faith and the religious definition of man, let alone the nature of scientific detachment and objectivity. Neither do the devotees of science show any clearer understanding of the existential ambiguities confronting man—those ambiguities which it is the proper responsibility of religion to clarify and which some think that science can and must dispel. There is no real conflict between the respective provinces of religion and science; whenever conflict appears, it is between false conceptions of these provinces, between a scientific conception of religion and a religious conception of science. That religion and science need not antagonize each other is the point of Bacon's remark to the effect that science leads to the insight and visions of faith, but a mere veneer of science does not.

Religion is to be blamed for a good deal of the animosity between science and itself. It often provoked science to rebellion. Christianity began to lose its authority, and *ipso facto* its relevance, as soon as it claimed to give a scientific account of man and the universe. And the thinly veiled dogmatism of the devotees of science is but a repercussion of the intransigence of Christianity in scientific matters. Like rationalism, scientific agnosticism is a natural child of Christianity. Even so, there is no opposition between religious truth and scientific truth, between the method of faith and the method of science. It is not the scientific achievements up to date which render the Christian faith inefficient. Here, as with authority, the worst dilemma of modern man stems from the fact that his whole life is spent in a search for consistency, for the principle of unification. It is a characteristic of the Christian view that man's experience lives on another level than that of logical consistency. When, in reacting against the progressive dissolution of its authority, Christianity began to desire consistency, it disowned the very foundations of the scientific quest it had itself laid down.

One of the significant aspects of classical Christianity (and of Judaism) is its understanding of the universe, of the world, or reality, or nature. From the point of view of Biblical thought, the universe is God's creation. Between these two realities—that of God and that of his creation—there is a concomitance which is so construed that God's reality cannot be deduced, either by addition or subtraction, from the reality of the creation. God's being is not the sum total of all beings; nor do other beings participate in the nature of God. And yet Biblical thought is audaciously anthropomorphic. It even pushes anthropomorphism to the extent that, Rudolf Bultmann points out, the divine is described in human terms while the human is appraised in divine terms. Yet God is never conceived as the ideal man, nor man as divine. When Adam wants to become like God, he "falls." There is a boundary between God and man, as there is between the Creator and the Creature or the Creation. This boundary does not exclude the fact that God is *man's* God, that between them there is a fundamental concomitance or reciprocity or mutuality. Accordingly, God can dwell in man, but he is not human; and he can manifest his presence through his creation, be present in it, but never become a part of it.

The concept of God as the Creator precludes both naturalism or spiritualism and mysticism or rationalism. All of these aim to provide man with a world-view which is primarily coherent—so coherent that God himself becomes a part of the universe which is to be explained. God thus becomes either the First Cause or the *Deus ex machina*. By contrast, the privilege of Biblical thought is that in its presentation, the explanation of the universe in its relation to man only serves as a pointer to God—to that without which the explanation could never be constructed, although the explanation does not abrogate the actual inconsistencies of existence. What Reinhold Niebuhr says of the Biblical myth applies to Biblical thought in general. One of its fundamental distinctions consists in "picturing the world as a realm of coherence and meaning without defying the fact of incoherence. Its world is coherent because all facts in it are related to some central source of meaning"[1]; but all facts are not immediately coherent and meaningful, because Biblical thought does not aim at formulating a system of rational or naturalistic unity.

God is neither the world-soul nor the zenith of human nonrational introspection, just as he is not the absentee landlord referred to as the *Deus ex machina*. But God stands over against man and confronts him, whether life is coherent or not and

whether destiny is woven with logical consisten-
cies or not. Otherwise man and his achievements,
as well as his shortcomings, would not draw their
meaning from a source beyond themselves; and
man would not be a creature but a demiurge of
one kind or another. The history of the world
would constitute a self-contained framework of
meaning. On the contrary, even as the meaning of
existence lies outside existence, in the dialectical
relatedness implied by the polarity between
Creator and creature, so also the meaning of
history lies above and beyond history. The Creator of the world is also he who sustains it and
gives it meaning. The Origin of history is also its
End. In the Judaeo-Christian point of view, the
concept of *telos* (*i.e.* of a divine purpose guiding
the human and historical facts of coherence as well
as of incoherence) means just that. Under no circumstances does Biblical thought reduce God to
either an intellectual or a moral principle directly
accessible to man within himself or without in nature and history, though he remain the God *of*
man, and *of* nature, and *of* history.

That is why in the thinking of Biblical religion
God's primordial attribute, underlying or coincid-
ing with his Creatorhood, is his capacity to reveal
himself. The Creator God is at the same time he
who reveals himself. God is not man, but the
source of the reality of man; between them there
is an infinite qualitative difference. "God is not
in nature; he is the Creator, the possibility of
nature. His silence may be in nature; but not his

speech. His hands and feet, perhaps, as Calvin said, but not his heart."[2] And God is not in history, but is the beginning and the end of it.

These views affect both the field of science and technology and the field of ethics, or existence as moral experience. In the last century or so both fields have systematically attempted to rid themselves of theological postulates and assumptions. Their efforts have been crowned with success. But this success is not without its ironical side: it was Christianity which emancipated them from their supernaturalistic bondage by setting them upon a course of independent inquiry.

What set them on this independent course was the Christian emphasis on the *radical contingency* of creation: one wonders at the fact that anything created *is;* that, rather than nothing at all, creation is. Therefore to find out what it is, one *looks to see,* rather than deducing the nature of the world from some principle or essences. The creation, which need not be, presumably could be *otherwise* than it is found empirically to be, without derogation upon the glory of the Creator. He had not to make the world, as Aristotle supposed, or history, as Spengler or Bergson or Toynbee suppose.

It was hopefully assumed, and with reason, that this inquiry would naturally culminate in the creature's participation in the universal concert of God's glorification. Such a position is not without foundation so long as one admits, as Christianity taught, that God is the possibility of scientific investigation as well as of nature; and that equally

God is the possibility of human behavior and consequently of social experiences and of cultural achievements. The irony was materialized as soon as science and ethics or art refused to return the compliment: they, indeed, could be without being the possibility of God. Modern humanism was thus born, with the primary aim of confining itself to the framework of the phenomenal world, since no noumenal world, if it exists, can be guaranteed other than through an act of surrender or through self-alienation. There arose in Western culture a scientific and anthropocentric humanism which, even in terms of Christian premises concerning the reality of this world, has not only succeeded in formulating a coherent view of the universe; it has also succeeded in rendering Christianity vulnerable precisely at the point where it would claim to be relevant to the condition of man and especially of modern man.

The Scientific Approach and the New Humanism

Christianity, in keeping with Biblical thought, could not equate God and nature, and therefore opposed all forms of nature worship as being essentially idolatrous. It confined itself to the transcendental, and it begot science as a method of investigation toward a descriptive understanding of nature and the universe. But Christianity was not always willing or ready to acknowledge in fact the position it was bound to assume in principle. Theology was granted the title of Queen of the Sciences, and a good deal of time was spent on assuring and promoting the hierarchical subordination of the other fields of knowledge. Sometimes science suffered not so much from its theoretical subordination to the fields of spiritual concern as from a human tendency to confuse the goals of science with those of religion. This kind of error occurred time and again. Samuel Johnson, for example, rejoiced in his *Memoirs* that similtaneously Berkeley, Hutchinson, and the Abbé Pluche came to the conclusion that the teaching of the Bible conferred upon man the knowledge of a truly natural philosophy as well as the knowledge of the only true religion. Johnson was confusing the realms of natural phenomena and of spiritual reality; he was confusing empirical fact and a transcendental understanding of its meaning. His preconception about the inextinguishable light that the Bible can shed on human problems and aspirations was founded on a pious lie. Nevertheless, Christianity was instrumental in setting up the foundations of modern science and all that derives from it in the fields of technology or even sociology and economics, in the independence it accorded to creation.

There was an irreducible ambiguity in the classical attitude of Christianity *vis-à-vis* science. This was a variant of the fundamental ambiguity that underlies all religiosity. Without this ambiguousness religion could not appeal to those aspirations in the nature of man which are the highest. But the same aspirations, or rather their object, to paraphrase Lawrence Durrell, often engage what is lowest in man.

The basic ambiguity in the Christian conception of science consisted in the claim that science should fulfill itself in the glorification of God. Properly speaking, this glorification was the business of religion. Science was thus set free—on a leash. Science was still subjugated to religion—to evoke the glory of God from a universe which religion conceived as God's handiwork. Science was denied any authentic independent purpose so long as its *raison d'être* was ancillary to the proper task of religion. But this is only the first layer of the ambiguity. There is a second. The subordination of science to religion reveals, by the ancillary rôle ascribed to science, the eminently religious preconception that there can be no world-view other than a religious one.

This is a reversal, perhaps unconscious but a reversal nonetheless, of the original Christian conviction that faith in the transcendent Creator and all conceptions of God as First Cause or clockmaker are mutually exclusive. Christianity betrayed this principle as soon as it attempted to become a self-consistent world-view. It turned into a speculative theory about life and the universe and quite expectedly forced itself on other ways of human intelligence and especially on science. Ceasing to be the question addressed to all the questions and answers about the meaning of the universe, it now posed as an imperialistic answer. It claimed to possess the knowledge of good and evil. And like Adam, it "fell." In its attitude *vis-à-vis* science, Christianity became a mere system. Vulnerable as all systems are, it was bound to live but the life of a system. Soon it was challenged. Science, which was allowed because it would aid the contemplation of God in the universe, now realized that this contemplation was purely incidental to its purpose and to its conquests. Christianity could have admitted this, were Christianity still abiding by the principle that God is not the missing link of a hypothesis.

Logic impelled science to discard what it considered coincidental or incidental, just as the same logic impelled Christianity to try to keep science under its thumb. Science no longer sought to decipher God's intelligibility in the world. It simply sought henceforth to understand the world itself. Here, too, there is a tinge of irony: the purpose of science became precisely that which, under the auspices of Christianity, had enabled it to come into being, namely the proposition that since the world was God's creation, it was worth investigating and understanding. Science even rendered an unexpected service to Christianity: it disabled naturalism, or nature worship, and obliterated it in such a way that it can no longer raise its head. Christianity could have expected this from the science which it had engendered.

But science did not do this in the name of the Christian God. It was by its nature indifferent to the particular type of religiosity it devalued. This devaluation was pure coincidence, and science was far from seeking it, just as it realized that it was not less scientific for not seeking to take part in the concert of God's glorification. Meanwhile, however, the *entente cordiale* between Christianity and science was becoming a source of real conflict.

The turning point occurred at the moment when the post-Christian era began. This turning point was brought about by science; it was not what science sought, but it soon became what science had brought to light. Its characteristic was that while science could neither prove nor disprove the existence of God, it attempted to explain the universe as a self-contained entity without necessarily having recourse to extraneous sources of meaning such as God. In a parallel way, man was no longer seen as owing allegiance to God in order to understand himself: the religious mode of self-knowledge, although authentic, no longer constituted the only authentic avenue. At the same time, the feeling of dependence on an absolute became a luxury and a superfluity, since man's knowledge of the universe, though quite relative, still was more certain than his knowledge of any absolute.

Before the turning point, man lived in an atmosphere where nature was conceived as being created by God. Now, however, nature is defined only in relation to man; man himself replaces God and, by assuming responsibility for the universe in which he lives, he not only dismisses God but also acts as a creator. When, in the name of this new creator, science seeks to evoke a coherent and self-consistent world-view, it is actually questing for the knowledge of good and evil: it intends to correct nature and remake the creation—in the name of man. At this point, science is no longer situated where at first it realized that God's hand in the universe, though perhaps a significant religious truth, is at best a superfluous bit of irrelevant conviction. It now constitutes itself as an alternative conception of the universe. It wills itself to be truly atheistic and humanistic.

This does not merely negate the Christian view; it wills to assume responsibilities for the incoherence as well as the coherence of the universe and those of humanity, hoping to correct incoherence by a laborious and patient research into what meaning of the evidence it can glean. This atheism succeeds in invalidating what Christianity had called revelation, since the world is no longer regarded as God's handiwork, as the revelatory mirror of God's creative act. The elimination of the concept of creation entails the elimination of the concept of revelation and, furthermore, that of a revealed religion. Nonetheless, even if distantly, something seems to recall a religious world-view: this atheism is technological or truly Promethean for the first time. This comes from the fact that science, while it dethroned both natural and revealed religion, had also broadened its scope and snatched from religion its age-old handmaid, art. Technology is the irrepressible result of this new alliance between science and art. (Perhaps no epithet better qualifies this post-Christian age than "technological.")

But the rise of scientific or atheistic humanism is not due solely to these developments taking place in scientific thought. This rise was also prepared by developments occurring within Christianity, perhaps as a result of the impact of science. Christianity was not aware of this dishabilitating impact, even though there are many historical cases, from Galileo on, which it handled very poorly. It was not on the level of such spectacular aberrations—a blunder may become a redeeming factor —that Christianity was most in danger, but on another, less official, level. The perilous moment was not a head-on collision between Christianity and science. The fatal blow came unexpectedly from a rather human and natural desire to unify science and religion, under one pretext or another and especially that of clinging to a religious view which had lost its relevance and was being superseded. "By the end of the nineteenth century," writes James H. Nichols, "revivalism had largely washed out of the churches theological education, ordered worship, and sacramental practice, and the new theology and ethics drew to a marked degree on sources extraneous to the faith, especially on popular science."[3]

At the same time, attempts to reconcile religion and science were taking place on a higher level than that of popular religion or popular science. From Locke's *The Reasonableness of Christianity* and Kant's *Religion Within the Limits of Reason* and far beyond into the beginning of the twentieth century, one thought seems to have preoccupied many theologians and philosophers, that of accounting for the validity of Christianity in accordance with the scientific and progressivistic predilections of the times. Especially many a Christian thinker wanted to be not only a Christian but also a *modern* man. From Friedrich Schleiermacher to Albrecht Ritschl this became so predominant a concern that often the Christian was sacrificed to *modern* man, and Christianity accommodated to the cultural exigencies of the period. These theologians differed from their atheist contemporaries. But they differed even more seriously from their predecessors.

From the perspective of classical Christian thought, the universe was a symbolic book pointing to God the Creator and Revealer, just as a cathedral is said to be a Bible in stone. Reason was not defined as conflicting with revelation, but was nonetheless endowed with a special privilege in its own sphere, independent of the sphere of faith. Between the terms of this duality there stood the figure of Christ holding them distinct but not separate, united but not confused.

By contrast, the theological constructions of the modern period give the impression that the universe is all the revelation there is of any God that may be; and that reason is but a more cogent and effective principle under which truth is grasped more adequately and less offendingly than under the principle of faith. In their legitimate effort to address the cultural despisers of religion (as Schleiermacher put it) these theologies reach the extreme of subsuming religion under a nascent scientific and technological culture. If nineteenth-century theologians did not borrow directly from highbrow science as revivalism did from popular science, they did attempt to placate it all they could, and to render Christianity less mysterious, less demanding, less religious, and correspondingly more cultural. Richard Niebuhr's judgment about the cultural theologians of that century describes this attempt:

Reason, they think, is the high road to the knowledge of God and salvation; Jesus Christ is for them the great teacher of rational truth and goodness, or the emergent genius in the history of religious and moral reason. Revelation, then, is either the fabulous clothing which intelligible truth presents itself to people who have a low I.Q.; or it is the religious name for that process which is essentially the growth of reason in history.[4]

Science was not alone in preparing the grounds for a self-reliant humanism. Christian theologians, too, were quite vocal in their attempts to show that Christianity was far from being adverse to it. A self-reliant universe and a no less self-reliant humanism became, for them, the highest manifestations of what formerly depended upon God's creative act and his redemptive purpose. All that was immanent and finite, yet susceptible of unlimited perfectibility, was naïvely regarded as the best incarnation of the transcendent and infinite. In the face of a world becoming self-contained and self-reliant, Christianity did not know quite what to do with a God who, more and more insufferably, had all the aspects of an intruder. Since Job the rôles had been reversed: the discoverers and conquerors of the world held a council, and God was propped up in their midst. But there was no Job.

The Ethic of Radical Immanentism

The inauguration of a post-Christian universe is to be imputed to the delinquency of Christianity rather than wholly to the arrogance of science or any other movement, materialistic or ideological, that Christians would like to construe as secularistic. Even if it intended to grapple with actual and not theoretically abstract problems confronting the concrete man of the nineteenth century, Christianity had intellectually misconducted itself, and forfeited its relevance. For the sake of winning the world, it lost its soul. This constant dilemma of Christianity was never more desperately urgent than to those who faced it with the embalmed corpse of a dead body of beliefs.

Christianity had not altogether ruled out the possibility, let alone the necessity, of reconciliation between faith in God and man's not unnatural desire to find meaning in the universe and see it objectively confirmed. But, traditionally, faith in God was itself the document confirming that there is meaning in the universe. In the modern period

Christianity began with a guileless but fatigued assent to the seemingly evidential confirmation of the meaningfulness of the universe and, taking this as a document, hoped to have it at least countersigned by God. God became but an appendix to the marvels and wonders of a scientific universe. The cart had been placed before the horse. And since then, those who still hold to the Christian faith have been trying to keep pace with the irresistible forces of a post-Christian era.

Every age molds man according to its own image. The mark of this post-Christian age is that it has lost the power of contemplation so necessary to the Christian world-view. Its motto seems to be: That is scientific and accordingly humanistic which, if it can be done, ought to be done, and if it ought to be done, can be done. The measure of all things, man claims for himself the privilege of being responsible for this world. But this he construes no longer in the sense in which Christianity understood man's responsible involvement in the world as a corollary to his commitment to God. His responsibility to this world is the only kind of commitment he knows and can justify. This justification follows the path of a reasoning which resembles the traditional Christian motif of a fallen universe needing God's redemptive action. But man himself is now assuming this divine prerogative. His responsibility toward the universe is to redeem it from the incoherent elements of which he claims himself innocent. This claiming of responsibility, Lacroix aptly remarks, is accom-

(181)

panied by a refusal to assume culpability. Contemporary atheism is largely a claiming of innocence, even as it is a vindication of humanism. It does not even bother to be antitheistic, since it does not undertake the problem of reconciling the presence of evil and suffering with the justice and the goodness of God.

The cornerstone of this post-Christian age is not an attempt to fit evil into a coherent view of the universe, but to eliminate it from the universe. How else could man's dominion over nature and its elements be concretely manifested? Man now is what Christ, according to the New Testament, was to the world. He is the new redeemer, the meaning-giving center of this post-Christian era. In Toynbee's warning, the danger today is not a re-emergence of nature-worship but the creeping religiosity of man-worship. Vincent van Gogh's burning desire, though quite susceptible to loftier aims, provides a zealous if ambiguous confirmation of this tendency to attribute to man what formerly was a divine quality. "I would," he said, "paint men and women with that eternal *je ne sais quoi*, of which a halo was once the symbol." Much less ambiguously, Sartre and Camus picture man as the only one worthy of governing that which is his own kingdom anyway, especially now that God has been finally persuaded to give up his protracted regency.

Just as Sartre and Camus are aware that the solution of old problems, even pseudo problems, only raises a new series of dilemmas, science and

(182)

humanism do not consider that the major questions have been answered. No doubt with a certain amount of malice, Sartre said in his short essay on existentialism that the absence of God does not make things any easier—on the contrary. One can no longer appeal to an ultimate seat of judgment and mercy to complete and correct in a heavenly realm what has been left incomplete and uncorrected on this earth. Just as it was difficult ever to be sure of precisely what the will of God entailed, so it is equally difficult to determine which image of man is going to govern man's responsibility for this world. The atomic bomb and the repression of the Hungarian uprisings are revelations of one image, even while the harnessing of the atom and the artificial satellites reflect another image. The will of man may be even more difficult to fathom than the will of God.

Modern man is in at least one respect as helpless and disoriented as Mary Magdalene, who stood weeping outside Jesus's apparently empty tomb "because they have taken away my Lord." The drive toward logical consistency has not, despite the success of its logic in eliminating God, achieved consistency where it matters most. No longer in need of God, modern man still needs to find himself. He is back where he started from. Previously his quest was undertaken under theistic auspices. It is now undertaken under post-Christian and sometimes atheistic auspices. The directions are no longer the same. They are no longer transcendental but purely immanental. Their meaning does not depend on a beginning in the action of a Creator God; nor does it depend on an end fulfilled by a divine intervention. It is neither at the foot nor at the top of Sisyphus's mountain; it is in the rock's subordination to Sisyphus. In the name of the Kingdom of God, Christianity negates any self-sufficient order cozily established in a self-reliant universe. But in the name of man, post-Christian thought denies the moral and spiritual certitudes invested in a Kingdom of God, and refuses them the task of ameliorating the deficient order evolved from an unreliable universe.

This post-Christian ethic presents characteristics analogous to the Christian. Like the Christian, it is primarily an ethic of solidarity. But here this solidarity is achieved only if God is excluded, for instead of cementing it, he would betray it. Kant notwithstanding, God has become superfluous as a postulate authenticating moral action. This ethic is thoroughly anthropocentric. It perhaps agrees with the Christian tradition about the universality of the law of nature; but unlike the Christian tradition, it does not regard the natural law as a prop for a theologically oriented ethic. Instead of considering the law of nature as implying the divine law, it regards that implication as a usurpation of the human order in favor of a divine order at best improbable and irrelevant.

The post-Christian ethic here diverges from the Christian to the point of opposing it radically. In the Christian view, Adam's fall simultaneously precipitated the corruption of the whole world.

The solidarity of mankind, on this account, is a corollary of its common sinfulness. Responsibility surges from the realization of guilt and its forgiveness by a divine intervention. By contrast, the post-Christian ethic establishes solidarity on the basis of man's innocence of the absurdity of the world. The great difference lies in this: the Christian ethic is an ethic of forgiveness; the post-Christian is an ethic of innocence. Because in each case responsibility is the essential cornerstone, the post-Christian ethic cannot be lightly dismissed on the pretext that it is merely a secularization, an amputated and negative version of the Christian. If anything, it does not propose to be easier than the Christian ethic. Neither optimistic nor self-complacent, it constitutes a serious challenge to the Christian view and a more authentic choice in a "desacralized" universe. Jean-Paul Sartre's play, *The Flies,* describes the present post-Christian situation as providing man with the only condition relevant to an authentic apprehension of his existence and his destiny. This situation is both a result of the Christian tradition and its ultimate negation. Modern man has been so fashioned by Christianity that he can only reject it in order to be himself.

JUPITER: I am not your King, impudent worm. Who then has created you?

ORESTES: You, but you should not have created me free.

JUPITER: I gave you freedom in order to serve me.

ORESTES: This may be so, but it turned against you and neither you nor I can do anything about it. . . . Nor am I excusing myself for this.[5]

Orestes further explains his attitude by declaring that Jupiter may be the king of gods as well as the king of stones and the stars, and the king of the waves of the sea, but he is not the king of man. So far as modern man is concerned, Christianity may be the only or the best religion, but it is not his religion. He will not forsake the world in order to find the meaning of the only existence to which he is bound, as he is to this world. And by forsaking Christianity, he finds that this world contains at least one meaning—that of human existence.

The life of a religion is to be measured by the efficacy of its symbols. A symbol, though it has an authenticity of its own and therefore imposes itself, yet may die. So, also, a religion.

The symbols of Christianity are all theocentric, as were the culture and the humanism they fostered. It is difficult to make them relevant to a milieu like the present one, which is impregnated by an atheistic and anthropocentric humanism. Even where religiosity survives, there also the concern is centered on man.

But the prevalent anthropocentrism of today does not signify that men are now more egotistical than their ancestors. Selfishness has always been equally and profusely distributed to all men in all ages. A man may believe in God for purely selfish reasons, often eloquently externalized as the fear of hell. That kind of selfishness at least has lost its appeal now that hell has become a questionable reality; or, rather, now that man is his own redeemer. The clear meaning of the present anthropocentrism is this: the improbability of God is a practical fact; it is an everyday reality available to the experience of all existing beings.

This, then, is the force of the ineluctably anthropocentric categories by which this age understands its situation. The death of God is not an intellectual cry of merely iconoclastic value. Nor was God's presence ever a matter of purely intellectual assertion or demonstration. As such it meant little, unless it was translated into concrete realities and concern. But God's absence, or the death of God itself, has become what a man directly experiences. It is no longer a theoretical declaration; it is a practical awareness by which authentic existence often is measured. The classical Christian who believed in God and lived accordingly was often incapable of intellectually arguing the existence of God. And, certainly, he did not have to demonstrate it with arguments and counterarguments. But this did not invalidate the reality of God—it was no less relevant to a man's concrete situation. What today's anthropocentrism expresses is the irrelevance of God—be he real or just an idea—to concrete existence. God is dead, not in sheer intellectual scaffoldings, but in the down-to-earth give and take of the human condition.

The era of God's death may be only a transition.

New social structures and cultural forces may pick up what Western culture has now deserted. Through the Pilgrim fathers, America picked up and re-enlivened the spirit of utopian and radical-Christian adventurousness when a disintegrating Christendom was torn by religious, economic, and nationalist strifes. The Pilgrims infused this spirit into a commonwealth which was all the more majestic because it implied a radical rupture with the past and a bold new beginning. Something of the sort is still theoretically conceivable; it seems, though, that such a recurrence is a matter of faith and hope rather than of an objective diagnosis, for in the present context Christianity has no strong foothold. It seems to have fulfilled its rôle and reached the point of obsolescence. Life is replete with such built-in obsolescent devices: they are discarded once they have accomplished their usefulness. And, again, the result is a radically immanentist conception of life.

If anything characterizes the modern temper, it is a radical immanentism. This immanentism is significant because scientifically and culturally as well as theologically it is impossible to identify God as prime mover or universal sustainer of the world of phenomena. Ethically, this immanentism prohibits reliance on any ready-made codes, whose enforcement depends on inquisitorial procedures or on obscurantist theologies. Consequently, it means going beyond the temporal and temporary realizations Christianity has bequeathed to the contemporary world. Irony reaches its climax

(188)

when even the Christian discovers that his God really is not the foundation stone of all that he had been accustomed to regarding as an integral part of a culture he termed Christian. This same Christian is then in the position where he must at least grant validity to the counterchoices proposed by a thoroughly immanental humanism. If the contemporary human predicament is not necessarily as the humanists and atheists describe it, the Christian view is even less self-evident and, in fact, its relevance is even more hypothetical. Thus, at the present juncture, the least that a Christian can and must do is to acknowledge the dichotomy, even antinomy, between the Christian ideal and the assumptions that gird the spirit of this de-Christianized world. Such an acknowledgment, minimal though it is, warrants the assertion that the post-Christian era has dawned.

CHAPTER IX

The Legacy of Christianity: Its Self-Invalidation

In pervading popular Christianity, radical immanentism has resulted in a cultural and religious incapacity for God; and in its involvement with Christian existentialism it has brought to light the contemporary Christian's total religious dilemma as, in order to be true to himself, he must face his—and our—culture's incapacity for the Christian God. In both cases, popular or existentialist, the radical monotheism of the ages of faith is giving way—shamelessly in the former, reluctantly in the latter—to the radical immanentism of our present culture.

The Radical Immanentism of Reliogisity

The ideals impregnating the contemporary climate of opinion are deceptively simple. Though people wear them differently, today as always, they embody the time-worn quest for peace and security, tranquillity and prosperity, both corporal and spiritual. Even the age-old dream has not varied: the lamb lying next to the lion is a favorite of the popular imagination. Because these ideals are so deceptively simple, Christianity today more than ever stumbles over them. For Christianity, as the popular mind conceives it, promises the realization of these ideals in the future, beyond this life. The present climate gravitates round their realization here and now. Though the concern has not changed, the means and the goal have; this makes these traditional ideals even more simple and deceptive. For example, the Declaration of Independence enumerates the inalienable rights of man as life, liberty, and the *pursuit* of happiness. Happiness it did not regard as a legitimate inalienable right. For the modern temper, however, happiness, whether inalienable or not, is a good by far superior to its pursuit. In theological terms, the contrast is even more striking. To recall Saint Augustine's famous declaration: *"Cor meum inquietum donec requiescat in te."* ("My heart is restless until it rests in thee.") The modern version abbreviates this declaration by the last two words, and proposes happiness no matter where it comes from, peace regardless of the means, life irrespective of the end. As Baudelaire said of beauty: *"Que tu viennes du ciel ou de l'enfer, que m'importe?"* ("Whether you come from heaven or hell, what does it matter to me?") And

Henry C. Link lined this feeling with religious self-assurance when he declared that "faith in fallacies is better than no faith at all." Link wrote this in his book *The Return to Religion,* published in 1936.

History is filled with irony. The fifties witnessed a return to religion, which was called "revival." It was neither a return nor a revival, but an illustration on a mass scale of Link's fallacious exhortation to take up religion. This illustration or, rather, this phenomenon was based on more refined and sophisticated appeals than Link's crude statement implied.

Whether this religious decade is considered from the point of view of the masses which were fascinated by its religious motifs or from the point of view of the inspirators of the revival, the religious density of the general sentiment had been diluted beyond recognition. The religion of the fifties at best was a more-and-more-of-less-and-less religion; at worst, it was a less-and-less-of-more-and-more religion. It was an age of faith in faith, of belief in belief; and all it achieved was to fill holes with other holes. Religion is a self-devouring monster.

It was therefore not surprising that people were prone to make hyperbolic professions of faith, or to be swayed by the succinctness of declarations that promised faith in capsule forms. "I believe—those two words with nothing added," Daniel Poling exclaimed, as though he were wondering, why bother with instant coffee? Just swallow the coffee bean. President Eisenhower once declared, no doubt meaning to impart wisdom, though probably beguiled by the sound of enticing but unfortunate words: "Our government makes no sense, unless it is founded in a deeply felt religious faith—and I don't care what it is." Both by tradition and by choice, the Puritan legacy and the Judaeo-Christian tradition from which this nation's character stems certainly would care what kind of faith it is, and in what. So, also, would a humanist, a man of culture.

In the previous chapter two symptomatic attitudes were analyzed, expressive of the transition from the Christian to a post-Christian era. The first was the technological, or scientific, mentality which so apprehends and construes this world that it is not innately endowed with a religious or divine dimension: whatever the meaning-giving center of this universe is, it cannot be called God. The second attitude largely depends on and sustains the first. It evolves from a plea of innocence with respect to evil and injustice, and proceeds toward an atheistic ethic of responsibility and decision designed to establish the initial perception of innocence. Thoroughly autonomous, neither legalistic nor antinomian, it is at the same time a rigorously anthropocentric ethic.

The revival of the fifties accords with both of these attitudes. Being a religious phenomenon of sorts, it did present a certain view of salvation. So far as its fundamentalist side was concerned, this view was patterned after the old-fashioned hellfire and brimstone objurgatory style. But for the most part, peace of mind, of soul, or just plain material success constituted adequate substitutes for the classical benefits of salvation. The literature of the revival flourished with admonition, exhortation, advice, or simply information destined to secure the realization of either view of salvation. What strikes most in that literature is its dependence on self-acquired know-how, its technological orientation: *how to* achieve this or that, here and now.

The transcendental dimension of classical Christianity also was concerned with the problems of here and now. But between it and the contemporary attitude a reversal has taken place. Some have called this reversal a secularization of the mainsprings of the Christian faith. However it is called, the result is an immanentist concern with the here-and-now. The extent of this immanentism and its opposition to the classical Christian doctrine can be expressed by a comparison of their attitudes toward faith. Faith without works is dead—this is the way Christianity understood the relation of faith, of trust in God, with human obligations unto this world and its complex reality. Religious existence was a mode of existence through which the world was *transfigured*, and with it all the pain as well as happiness it can offer. In the mentality of the revival there is an entirely different perspective. Religion is good, or faith is a good thing, because it works. And it works really only if the perplexing realities of this world are not transfigured but subjugated. Their subjugation is itself the test of a faith that works. Faith is gauged by the rewards of this life. In contrast, in the highest moments of Christianity those who put their trust in God and construed this as the key to the meaning of existence both grew spiritually and—adventitiously—happened to prosper mentally and materially as well. The recent temper of religiosity and the classical Christian tradition stand at extreme opposites. Neither purity of faith nor purity of heart matters so much as the *efficiency* of some religious system or another—so long as it produces material wealth or, a more fashionable substitute for wealth, mental if not physical health. Norman Vincent Peale, to name one of the high priests of the new religiosity, wrote in a jargon candidly borrowed from the ideology of business organization: "Today any successful and competent businessman will employ the latest and best-tested methods in production, distribution, and administration, and many are discovering that one of the greatest of all efficiency methods is prayer power." Prayer is money.[1]

This phenomenon shows that the secularization of Christianity has not been accompanied by an obliteration of the religious sentiment. In its lowest forms this sentiment has multiplied into a teeming "religionitis." Contemporary religiosity is thus neither Christian nor merely secularistic: it is idolatrous and constitutes a denial of Christianity.

What is the meaning of this transformation?

From the standpoint of Biblical religion the antithesis to faith is not involvement in secular responsibilities or obligations, but *idolatrous concern* about secular matters. Though faith in God is all-encompassing and concerns itself with all aspects of human existence, it can nonetheless show *lack* of faith in the way it voices its concern. Faith in faith, or religiosity, tends to substitute this concern for God himself, and thus idolatrizes it. The so-called revival of the fifties entailed and corroborated more than the mere secularization of Christianity; it betokened the *idolization* of religion. Two enlightened and compassionate authors, whose perspective was not primarily theological but sociological, write in a footnote to their sociological observations:

It is an intriguing speculation that, when faith lapses, the things it may ordinarily achieve for us without any particular thought or effort on our part become objects of technologically oriented behavior. The speculation is of interest both within and outside religion. It has been suggested that preoccupation with the technology of sexual intercourse is likely to occur when love has become a problematic and dubious matter, as well as that technologies of child-bearing appear when "natural" love for children is no longer an early and spontaneous thing. Similar considerations may apply in the field of religion. If this kind of speculation has any merit then the very emergence of a technological orientation in certain fields of human concern may be interpreted as in some sense a sign of degeneration.[2]

The nascent religiosity of this post-Christian era provides evidences of a technological orientation which are beyond dispute. From the inspirational book to Peale's elucubrations in *Look* magazine, the literature of this technological religiosity contains a number of suggestions for all kinds of do-it-yourself divine providence and predestination and salvation. By these means, lip service still was paid to the God of Christianity. Of equal merit, or demerit, are the similar suggestions which clutter the "mental science" strain characteristic of one side of the recent religiosity. But whether peace of mind and health are loftier goals of the religious life than wealth or success is of minor significance. Of greater importance is the technological apparatus which, with its precision for minutiae, equips both strains of religiosity. The subconscious stresses of popular religiosity underscore a certain consanguinity between religion and reason.

Technological religiosity represents, if not a clear victory of reason over faith, an unmistakable *abdication* of faith to reason—or unreason. It accommodates the fear and trembling as well as the unconditional trust normative of Christian existence to an inflationary mode of religious existence boasting a consistency which is only pseudological. This accommodation was so awkwardly carried out that the religion of the revival seemed to have run out of reasons for believing in God. Small wonder, then, that it should idolatrize peace of mind and similar substitutes. The fact that it did this by appealing to psychology or psychotherapy or technology or science by no means minimizes the adulteration of traditional Christianity. Actually, this adulteration is a sign of the elimination of Christianity from the very domain of religious manifestations. The desperate appeal to, or reliance upon, corroboration from extraneous sources are new-fangled crutches for a crippled religiosity claiming to stand for Christianity; such an alliance can be looked upon as a sign of lapse of faith. In the words of Jeremiah: "In vain you have used many medicines; there is no healing for you."

What did the revival accomplish? And of what, in the first place, was it a revival? There are two possible answers.

First, popular religiosity is, as it always will be, a maze. This is true in any case which involves the rather loose reality referred to as "the masses." Whether the religiosity under consideration is Christian or non-Christian, pre-Christian or post-Christian, it is always just amorphous enough to prevent any self-righteous judgment upon it. As Schneider and Dornbusch suggest in their study of inspirational books in America: "Perhaps above all else, the literature gives a powerful impression that the search for the philosopher's stone has not ended; it has only taken on new form and is carried on under new circumstances. The market for magic still appears to be very much alive, as it presumably was in far antiquity."[3] Difficult as it may be to imagine, from this angle, Christianity was not the prime beneficiary of the revival. On the

(198)

other hand, one is justified in raising the question whether the traditional pragmatism of American religion was not the logical generator of the technological orientation shown by the revival. If so, it is Christianity which engendered the monster that is devouring it now. By nature pragmatism can easily evolve into immanentism. When this happens, it paralyzes either faith in God or theism, *i.e.* Christianity, and levels everything down. In this case, everything was leveled down to the common denominators of a civic religion, the threefold religion of democracy which retained externally something of Judaism, of Catholicism, and of Protestantism.

Second, the idea of faith (to borrow Troeltsch's expression) has triumphed over the content of faith. Religiosity has triumphed over Christianity, because Christianity has lost its original value. This religiosity has neutralized all the symbolic and sacramental worth of the original Christian understanding of creation. It is peculiar to a self-reliant universe, although it contradicts this universe from the point of view of science itself. Despite all its claims, and especially its tacit assumptions, this is not a piety which bridges the gap between religion and science: pseudoreligious as well as pseudoscientific, it is the religion of scientism. It cannot address any authentic word to the cultural situation of this century.

It is difficult not to regard the recent resurgence of religiosity as but another in a series of Christian capitulations. Many times since the Reformation Christianity has known defeat, now by trying to recognize the contemporaneous conjuncture of religious and cultural realities, now by flagrantly refusing to recognize it. Schleiermacher's contemporaries were the intellectual and "cultured despisers of religion" whom Christianity had lost. From the characters of Dostoevski to Camus, Christianity has alienated those who seek justice. With Kierkegaard, the accommodation of Christianity to cultural relativities and misalliances was beginning to mean its cultural death, which Nietzsche was prompt in formulating. Perhaps more significant is the loss of the laboring masses in the nineteenth century, to whom Christianity remained callous, to the greater profit of Marxism. Today Christianity is losing the religious masses: this is the meaning of the revival of interest in religion. Christianity is losing these masses to an amorphous amalgam which includes elements from Christianity, from Judaism, and, in some spheres, from Zen Buddhism. It is this combination which benefited most by the revival.

Following Martin E. Marty's lead, it is interesting to compare this revival with the Great Awakening of the mid-eighteenth century, even though the former is not purely a Protestant phenomenon. The Great Awakening, as Robert Ellis Thompson remarked in 1895, "terminated the Puritan and inaugurated the Pietist or Methodist age of American Church History." It marked the transition from an emphasis on the sovereignty of God to one on the perfectibility of man, self-salvation, and progress. Some of the observations made in the preceding chapter show the parallelism between the transformation of American Protestantism and what affected Christianity in general elsewhere. The revival of the nineteen fifties, Martin E. Marty adds, in his book on *The New Shape of American Religion,* "is terminating the Pietist age and inaugurating . . . a post-Protestant age." Both times, argues the author, who is concerned chiefly with Protestantism, classical Protestantism was seriously defaced and lost some of its nerve. Each time, as well as during various intermediate revivals, it abdicated some of its essential tenets. And this time it has capitulated to the Baals of religiosity, the principal characteristic of which are a packaged God, interchangeable and mass-tailored man, and togetherness instead of true community. Recognizing the corrosive power of these characteristics, Marty warns that Protestantism must face one major fact in this new situation: that while "the 'old shape' of American religion was basically Protestant . . . , whatever else it includes, the 'new shape' of American religion is not basically Protestant."[4]

To combat this new-look religiosity, Marty, being concerned with Protestantism, suggests remedies and a strategy for a counteroffensive, generally consisting of a return to the sources—Biblical faith and classical Protestantism. Catholics would probably prefer Saint Thomas and the Counter Reformation to Luther and Calvin. Either way, the dilemma is the same. It evolves from the urgent need of a theological renascence which, for the sake of the present world, would clarify the Biblical meaning of God, man, and community. The problem is not so simple. The Reformation of the sixteenth century as well as the Counter Reformation took place in a dissimilar context. Whether ecclesiastical or social, spiritual or secular, the structures they affected, rearranged, or redefined were the embodiment of a Christian purpose and way of life. The novelty of the situation affecting American religion today is not merely its post-Protestant aspect, which is but a concomitant of another development afflicting the whole of Christianity. In America as elsewhere, the entire cultural setting is that of a post-Christian era. More than the ceremonies and rituals are put into question. As the ersatz religiosity of the nineteen fifties put into evidence, the Christian faith itself has been undermined.

There is a relation between do-it-yourself religiosity and the revendication of innocence typical of non-Christian humanism. Ultimately, both are anthropocentric and immanentist. The former deals in packaged gods, the latter, in the packaged man. Is this a coincidence? Perhaps not. The death of God has been the religious "heresy" of the West, and the disappearance of the hero—a theme dear to Colin Wilson—has been its cultural counterpart. The religiosity of modern man and the facelessness of the modern crowd are both expressions of the same heresy—call it religious or secular. But today's heresy often is tomorrow's orthodoxy.

This is the age of the post-Christian heresy. Only falsely heretical postures—such as togetherness, collectivism, individualism, conformism— only these die, because like God, they "make such a powerful appeal to what is lowest in human nature."[5] The revival of the nineteen fifties was the *religious* inauguration of the post-Christian era.

Existentialism and the Death of God

Christian existence is by nature dilemmatic. It must oscillate between two poles: homogeneity with the posture and condition of this world, on the one hand; heterogeneity to them, on the other. In Saint Paul's classic passage: ". . . the appointed time has grown very short; from now on, let those who . . . mourn [live] as though they were not mourning, and those who rejoice as though they were not rejoicing, and those who buy as though they had no goods, and those who deal with the world as though they had no dealings with it" (I Corinth 7/29-31). Christian existence must be qualified by homogeneity with the world, yet it must be *defined* by an irreducible heterogeneity to the world. To paraphrase Jesus, the scene of its unfolding is laid *in* this world, but its meaning and its purpose are not *of* this world. The dilemma is heightened by the fact that the same act of existence must be both homogeneous with the world and heterogeneous to it.

Kierkegaard manifested this concern when he wrote:

Luther says somewhere in one of his sermons that properly sermons should not be preached in churches. This he said in a sermon, which surely was delivered in a church, so that he did not say it seriously. But it is true that sermons should not be preached in churches. It harms Christianity in a high degree and alters its very nature, that it is brought into an artistic remoteness from reality, instead of being heard in the midst of real life, and that precisely for the sake of the conflict (the collision). For all this talk about quiet, quiet places and quiet hours, as the right element for Christianity is absurd.

So then sermons should not be preached in churches but in the streets, in the midst of life, of the reality of daily life, weekday life.[6]

The Christian promoters of the revival intended to do just that when they took Christianity to Yankee Stadium, or inserted it in the profane pages of a magazine, or displayed it through the picture tubes of television sets. They deemed it not incongruous that Christianity should be paraded among the articles by which the world frantically gratifies itself. The alliance between piety and Madison Avenue made itself heard in the heart of market places and business centers. There, the hidden persuaders of the Christian persuasion soon realized that the average man is generally the prey of innumerable worries, and wants nothing more than to be freed from them and to relax. Such was the demand—it always is. It was supplied—something always poses as an antidote to any kind of malaise. In the process, Christianity

(204)

ceased to abide by the law of its heterogeneity to the world, and became "exactly the opposite of what it is in the New Testament." To borrow again from Kierkegaard, the persuaders succeeded in cheating God out of Christianity. What else could they do in an age which cannot in the least grasp the reality of the Christian God? No other apostasy from Christianity could have been more tragic, more pathetic.

Another of Kierkegaard's invectives comes to mind. In the *Concluding Unscientific Postscript* he wrote: "In an age when the progress of culture and the like has made it seem so easy to be a Christian, it is quite in order to seek to make it difficult, provided one does not make it more difficult than it is." He added these words, which can apply only *indirectly* to the users of mass religiosity: "But the greater a man's equipment of knowledge and culture, the more difficult it is for him to become a Christian."[7]

Kierkegaard's meaning is not betrayed when his words, in order to underline their application to the present context, are altered in this way: The greater a man's equipment of pseudo knowledge and pseudo culture, the easier it is for him to become a pseudo-Christian. The reason as well as the intention of such an alteration can be justified by pointing to the idiosyncrasy of popular religion, namely, the immanentism which is the basis of both its technological orientation and its "scientism" (*i.e.* the concealed assumption that religion does not contradict science and the corresponding clear emphasis on the material, spiritual, or mental *efficiency* of religion). An immanentist Christian can only be a pseudo-Christian. He points in the same breath to his God and to his success. Kierkegaard justifies the use to which his invective is put—"the god that can be pointed out is an idol, and the religiosity that makes an outward show is an imperfect form of religiosity."[8]

The moral harks back to the dilemmatic characteristic of Christianity. The natural framework of a sermon is not the shielded sanctity of a church, but the market place, or main street, or whatever the elements by which a man identifies himself. Yet when Christianity surrenders to the pressures, or espouses the scale of values, of the market place, it forfeits itself and degenerates into an "imperfect form of religiosity." If the preacher concerns himself only with proclaiming the gospel to his congregation and does this within the protective walls of the church and its dogmas and rituals, soon there may not be much connection between what goes on in the remoteness of the sanctuary and the spiritual as well as material actualities of life. Both culturally and theologically, Christianity has always been faced with these two dangers. Most of the argument of these pages has dealt with the cultural aspect of this danger. It is time to deal now with its theological aspect.

Theology is the critical as well as self-critical function of the church. The church can perform this function in two ways which are fundamental to all others. These ways refer to different methods by which the church defines its mind; they also determine the nature of its critical and self-probing function. This function is conceived principally either as kerygmatic or as apologetic.[9] *Kerygmatic* is derived from a Greek word which means proclamation (like that of a herald); *apologetic* comes from another Greek word which means defense and vindication of a position, a situation, a fact, or a truth. In either theological method the strategy and the purpose are the same —to assess and impart the truth of Christianity. But the tactics are different. Kerygmatic theology satisfies itself with the proclamation of its truth and hopes that those who have ears will hear. Apologetic theology seems rather willing to come down into the arena and there to engage in a dispute, hoping that any rational man will soon be convinced of its truth. Each theological method relies a little on the other's position. The kerygmatic thelogian assumes that his words and concepts will be understood, while the apologist is in effect arguing for the intellectual or rational cogency of the truth he, too, is proclaiming. Paul Tillich (who is an apologist concerned with the proclamation of the Christian faith) would probably agree that every kerygmatic theologian, tacitly, is an apologist; likewise, every apologist is a kerygmatic theologian, sophisticatedly.

The danger confronting this twofold function of the church is always there. The danger of apologetic theology is that it identifies the specific truth of the Christian faith with whatever seems to attract the imagination at a given time. By deliberately making it "attractive," the apologist often evacuates this truth of its offensive yet not less essential elements. Christianity thus becomes the glorified version of every cultural and intellectual whim and fancy. The danger of kerygmatic theology is that it may cease to address itself to man's real condition; it may neglect to be contemporaneous with man's situation, except insofar as this situation is that of a man who is a member of the church. Karl Barth's teaching offers an excellent example of kerygmatic theology, published under the suggestive title of *Church Dogmatics*.

The foregoing comments on these two theological methods are not a digression; they are necessary to a discussion of existentialism, particularly of theological existentialism, some trends of which have adopted the apologetic method. Quite a few thinkers see in the alliance between existentialism and theology a signal opportunity to address the message of Christianity to the actual situation of modern man.

The juxtaposition of popular religiosity and existentialism is not meant to downgrade existentialism. There is a kinship between them. Existentialism is to Christian thought as popular religiosity is to the idea of Christian culture. It was an existentialist theologian, Paul Tillich, who ventured the careful opinion that not everything is bad in the attitudes of religiosity: at least they express a latent if not articulate concern.

What is intended here is not an examination of

the major existentialist systems. This would be extraneous and superfluous to the purpose. The concern is not centered on what is peculiar and significant about this or that system, or about this or that concept characteristic of a thinker. Rather, the concern is centered on those elements of the existentialist climate which are relevant as an illustration of the thesis that this age is post-Christian. Kierkegaard's own remark is quite appropriate here. He said, concerning existential concepts, that the desire to avoid definitions is proof of tactfulness. Indeed, there are as many existentialisms as there are existentialist philosophers.

What is relevant here is the fact that existentialism owes a particular debt to Christianity. Its origins are Christian. They are found in the writings of the Dane Sören Kierkegaard, for whom the basic problem was: How to become a Christian. This single theme, reinforced with the proposition that truth is subjective, or that subjectivity is the truth, unites all his works and unifies the multiple aspects of his thought. A number of other writers like Pascal and Augustine or Dostoevsky can be cited as parents of the existentialist movement. The list can be extended. Most significant is the opposition of Kierkegaard and Nietzsche, of the mood if not necessarily the content of their writings. In the firmament of existentialism, they have become almost inevitable luminaries. If Kierkegaard dealt with the problem of becoming a Christian, Nietzsche dealt with the problem of becoming a man. For both, this task was all the more urgent because it must be accomplished against a background of death. For Kierkegaard, Christianity is dead: so dead that Kierkegaard would not call himself a Christian. For Nietzsche, God is dead: it makes no sense to be a Christian if one has not prepared for the test of being a man—and the latter would exclude the former.

An unsuspected meaning of Nietzsche's cry is that the absence of God corresponds to Kierkegaard's view of the infinite qualitative difference between God and man. Both these views were expressed at a time when the drive toward immanentism was most irrepressible. Over against the picture of Jesus as the ideal man, and over against the idea of God as the consciousness of one's absolute dependence, Kierkegaard and Nietzsche at least withstood the leveling forces of immanentism. At the same time they had no alternative but to acknowledge the exclusion of God from the framework of a self-sufficient universe and a self-reliant humanism. To say that God is dead or to assert an infinite qualitative difference between God and man means not only that no ladder leads from man to God; it also means that there is no identity of substance between man and God, and, accordingly, that the problem of human existence is independent of the problem of God. Even as science, whatever its hypothesis, makes it impossible to identify this hypothesis with God, so also existentialism makes it impossible to identify God and man. The reality of man does not, logically or essentially, preclude the latter. That is why Kierkegaard could remain a Christian—but on the basis of the ancient formula: *credo quia absurdum.*

Existentialism is related to Christianity in the same way as technology is. Neither is thinkable without the Christian culture which originated them. But both flow into the stream of immanentism which runs opposite to the stream of classical Christianity. This awareness was Kierkegaard's thorn in the flesh. As Hohlenberg has said, Kierkegaard is the lovelorn lover of the religious. He is not a believer in the ordinary sense. He is a man of faith, but so desperately that his faith doubts itself and approves itself only when doubt leaps into faith.

Faith, for Kierkegaard, is not a fact. Nor is it a state. Rather, it is a constant becoming. It is an act, like a leap. But since Jesus is not the ideal man, and God is infinitely remote from man, even when from a religious interpretation he is nearer to man than man is to himself, there is no standard by which the act of existence can be measured *and* automatically authenticated. There is no law, except the exigencies of love and faith; and these cannot be erected into statutes.

Faith is a constant becoming, and is constantly exposed to doubt and despair. Similarly, existence is a constant becoming, and is constantly exposed to death. Throughout his life, man lives his death: "to die and yet not to die." But "the torment of despair is precisely this, not to be able to die." "Even the last hope, death, is not available . . . But this is an impossibility; the dying of despair transforms itself constantly into a living. The despairing man cannot die; no more than 'the dagger can slay thoughts' can despair consume the eternal thing, the self, which is the ground of despair . . ."[10] (Kierkegaard). In faith, the self becomes itself, that is, it becomes that which it is *not:* the sinful man becomes justified, even while only the justified man can realize the extent of his sinfulness. The self is a dialectic element between life and death, between possibility and necessity, or between finitude and infinitude. Essentially, the self is freedom for the reason that if existence is becoming, it involves an act, a choice, a decision grounded in freedom. It is not surprising, therefore, that Kierkegaard should have qualified existence as the "dizziness of freedom."

But freedom is not merely self-authenticated. It is also authenticated by the power of another self, or the other. Freedom is the other. For Kierkegaard it is, especially, the relatedness to the infinitely other—God. The self is "a relation which relates itself to another." As a relatedness, the self is a mode of being, in which it can be at one with itself just as it can be estranged from itself. Accordingly, Sartre echoes Kierkegaard when he writes in *No Exit:* "A man is what he wills himself to be." This is where the theistic existentialism of Kierkegaard still reverberates in the atheistic strains of contemporary existentialism.

It is also the point where existentialism no longer needs its theistic apparatus and can cast it off as one throws away crutches at the end of convalescence. If a man is what he wills himself to be, this means primarily that he has no justification *of his own* for what he becomes. Even in Kierkegaard's view, according to which the self is constituted by its transparent grounding in the power of God, the sinner who constantly is in need of justification can only thank *God's* justification, without which the sinner could not become what he is not, *i.e.* justified. Thus the Christian can appeal to God and rely on God's justification. For Sartre, no such privilege is available to man, since God is dead. And although man cannot justify himself—only heroes can do that; and life, as Olga says in *No Exit*, was not created to furnish man with occasions for heroism—man must nonetheless assume the responsibility of his acts, of becoming what he wills himself to be. Thus, he is sentenced to be free. Abraham felt he was sent by God. There is no one, Sartre contends, by whom one may claim to have been sent.

This is the situation in which man exists and must exert his freedom. There is no other situation, even as there is no other freedom. Because of this, man is free and responsible. And he is guilty because of it (because any act of freedom involves not only the agent but also all men). "Concrete humanity is the totality of its contradictions." Through the contradiction, man becomes free. Freedom is also threatened by the contradiction within as well as without the self: "Hell is other people."

But I know at least that I am. I adapt for my own use and to your own disgust, your prophet's foolish words: "I think, therefore I am" which used to trouble me sorely, for the more I thought, the less I seemed to be; and I say: "I am seen, therefore I am." I need no longer bear the responsibility of my turbid and disintegrating self: he who sees me causes me to be; I am as he sees me. I turn my eternal shadowed face towards the night. I stand up like a challenge, and I say to God: Here I am. Here I am as you see me and I do not know myself. What can I do except support myself? And you whose look eternally creates me, do support me. Mathieu, what joy, what torment! At last I am transmuted into myself. Hated, despised, sustained, a presence supports me to continue thus forever. I am infinite and infinitely guilty. But I *am*. Mathieu, I am. Before God and before men I am. *Ecce homo.*[11]

Existence is, in Martin Heidegger's word, *Dasein;* it means "being there," irrespective of who, supreme power and being or not, put one there. Man is thrown into such a situation, and he must assume all its conditions, all its finitude as well as its possibility. Man exists; that is to say, he is in a world "which is already given with his existence." Yet he is not quite at home in this world. He is, to quote the Biblical tradition, like a stranger and pilgrim on the earth.

John Macquarrie writes: Existentialism "is nothing other than a partial rediscovery of some aspect at least of the biblical understanding of man."[12] As this book plainly spells out, existentialism is related to Christianity in a special way, to which Rudolf Bultmann and Paul Tillich have been particularly sensitive. There are advantages as well as disadvantages in the existential approach to the meaning of the Christian faith. The affinities between Christianity and existentialism make it worth the venture. The affinities revolve around the fact that the first stage of an existentialist system deals with a phenomenological analysis of the human condition. The construction can then be fittingly completed and adapted to the exigencies of a Christian frame. It would be as if the existentialist analytic method had posed questions, and the answers depended on a religious—in this case Christian—orientation. The analysis would point to the Christian interpretation, and even necessitate it. Seemingly, all that is needed is the correlation of the existentialist problematic and the Christian revelation.

On this ground, it is conceivable to defend the Christian use of existentialism. The latter does analyze the condition of man in a manner sympathetic, if not homogeneous with, the New Testament concept of man. This is true even about the atheistic, or agnostic, side of the existentialist coin. Sartre, for example, deliberately uses terms and concepts that once were religious but which he has emptied of their Christian meaning while carefully preserving their emotional connotations. "Hell" and "guilt" are loaded words. They have religious overtones in any Western man's imagination. From this perspective, existentialism is unquestionably a form of religiosity. It has often the quality of a religious philosophy, as though it were nostalgic about the religious dimensions of a former existence. Sartre has protested against the evidences of such a longing; but he himself is not less vulnerable, despite the complaint he registered in *L'Etre et le Néant* that Heidegger's metaphysical inclinations cover up a desire to reconcile his humanism with the religious notion of the transcendent.[13] And Bultmann does corroborate this by providing Heidegger's philosophy with a religious, a Christian, complexion. At this very point, however, the advantages tend to turn into disadvantages.

When Bultmann borrows from Heidegger's philosophy, he does so not merely because it has religious undercurrents. His reason is somewhat more radical. For him, first of all, the task of the theologian is to communicate the Christian message to his contemporaries, even if this means that philosophy must be accorded antecedence over theology. Bultmann unambiguously admits that it does. Therefore, he adds, one might as well exert caution in choosing the best philosophical system available at a given time, since that is where one may find a contemporary image of man's self-understanding. It is better to indulge in such an attitude deliberately than involuntarily or unknowingly to remain in the dependence of a philosophical outlook which, though not being clearly recognized as such, is extraneous to the language of the New Testament.

(2 1 6)

Secondly, in order to communicate the Christian message to modern man in terms of his own situation, the theologian must begin by isolating the content of this message; he must sift it from the cultural, temporal, and temporary characteristics with which it was recorded in the New Testament. So far many theologians would agree with Bultmann. But, unlike most of them, Bultmann does not stop at defining the core of the Christian message. He takes what some (*e.g.* Barth) consider the fatal step: even this core, Bultmann argues, is dependent upon a world-view which is by and large superannuated today. This core must be rethought and reformulated for the sake of modern man.

Thirdly, the world-view of the New Testament is thoroughly mythological. In 1941 Bultmann startled the theological world by publishing the text of a conference now known under its second title, *Neues Testament und Mythologie.* In it he set the problem in the following terms: not only is the New Testament world-view mythological, but the core of its message also is mythological. According to the New Testament (which, in this case, shows how religious truth depends upon the ambient philosophical conceptions) the universe is composed of three stories: heaven above, the underworld down below, and the earth in the middle. The Gospel is full of references to angels and demons, Satan and supernatural powers. On the other hand, the representation of God's redemptive activity corresponds to these mythological views rather closely. God sends his son. This son was pre-existent and, though divine, he appears as a man. He is crucified, he dies and descends into hell. He rises again from the dead and ascends into heaven. Bultmann's conclusion is simple and unambiguous: it is impossible to adopt such a mythological conception of the world for contemporary usage. Faith should not be confused with, nor should it demand assent to, a mythological world-view or a mythological understanding of human nature. If the gospel is endowed with any truth, this truth must be independent of now irrelevant mythological conceptions. Otherwise, it would not make sense to hope to send a man into space or to the moon and believe at the same time that heaven is up above and hell is down below.

Besides, the tripartite division of the universe corresponds to past soteriological concerns, which envisioned man as well as the earth as a battleground of antagonistic supernatural forces of light and darkness, of good and evil. Man now thinks of himself as a "unified being," an integral personality. He understands himself and wills to assume responsibility for all he feels, thinks, and does. He ceases to understand himself when he becomes divided—a schizophrenic. He cannot be expected to subscribe to the New Testament views of the universe, of redemption and self-understanding, without violating the self-understanding he has achieved independently of the New Testament's archaic mode of apprehension.

Such violation would be equivalent to a denial of the intrinsic truth of the Christian message. If this truth would be inextricably bound up with notions and concepts which have been invalidated and discarded, and if such notions and concepts are irrelevant to the condition of modern man, so then would Christianity be irrelevant to this age.

When he speaks of the thought of the New Testament as a mythical type of thought, Bultmann does not mean ideology, as in twentieth-century practice we are inclined to mean. Nor does he mean that mythical thought, for being primitive, is not valid, or has little validity. Bultmann contrasts mythical thought with scientific thought. The former can be animistic, or super-naturalistic, or transcendentalist. The latter is characteristic of any type of reflection which presupposes that the universe is a closed entity, self-reliant if not always self-explaining, and that it is basically unified and draws its meaning from itself. This cannot be said about mythical thought: it tends to set up its understanding of human nature in terms of divine interventions; it speaks of the divine in human terms; and it signifies that neither the universe nor man can be understood in terms of an immanentist reduction. Thus, to break the mythological barrier of the New Testament world-view means essentially to make Christianity relevant to the present world. Modern man is conditioned by scientific loyalties that outweigh the primitive veracity of the Christian myth. He does not lift up his eyes to the hills from whence his help might

come (Psalm 121). The important thing, Bultmann contends, is to realize what kind of world-
view commands today's way of life: it is a world-
view determined by science and widely propa-
gated by the schools and the communications
media, and above all by technology.[14]

At the juncture of Bultmann's method and the
existentialist analysis there lies the fact that Western culture has gone from one kind of epochal
self-understanding to another. This coincides with
the translation from a sacral to a secular basis of
cultural values, from a theistic to an atheistic
universe—rather that merely from a mythical to a
scientific world-view. Bultmann would like to
think that the existentialist framework somehow
partakes of this scientific picture of the universe
and is at the same time a continuation, a revalori-
zation of mythical thought. Bultmann can retort
that the process of demythologization is an inner
necessity of the very meaning of the myth itself.
He can even add that this process is nothing new;
that everyone who reads and thinks about the
Bible and appropriates its meaning for himself
actually engages in demythologization; and that
the radical methods of nineteenth-century liberalism as well as the science of comparative religions had succeeded in two such attempts. Evidently, all this is correct. But it is correct only
within a specific framework. It is correct within
that framework which is operating still either
under the aegis of a primitive mythological
thought or under its sequel, the aegis of a sacral

impregnation of culture as well as a sacramental conception of nature. Certainly traces of the age-old attitudes still survive. But who can affirm that space-bound man will be the same as the earth-bound specimen that has so far occupied the scene? (Some even contend that, when man conquers space and other planets, he might well undergo physiological transmutations, along with an intellectual and spiritual reappraisal of his self-understanding.) Bultmann's enticing radicalism and his brave honesty at times seem like the compassionate attempt of a vestigial Christian who persists in applying the Christian view of creation to a world settled comfortably in its thoroughgoing immanentism, and in applying the Christian meaning of existence to the atheistic anatomy of post-Christian man.

Barth, in his controversy with Bultmann, claims that faith entails the acceptance of the core of the New Testament message; once this core has been isolated, it cannot be manipulated lest it is brought into subservience to a philosophical system and thus is denatured. Bultmann's objection to this position is simple, clear, and consistent: *sacrificium intellectus!* "The act of faith," he alleges, "is simultaneously an act of knowing, and, correspondingly, theological knowledge cannot be separated from faith."[15]

What Bultmann means is that, like Pauline theology, the core of the Christian message "deals with God not as He is in Himself but only with God as He is significant for man, for man's responsibility and man's salvation," just as it sees the world and man always in their relation to God. Therefore, to raise a question about God's act means to concern oneself with the question of human existence. To this extent, then, "theology is, at the same time, anthropology."[16] The adverbial phrase "at the same time" is of capital significance: Bultmann does not say with Feuerbach that theology *is* anthropology. But he sees the relevance of the former in its application to the latter, as he sees the meaning of the latter in its reference to the former.

Bultmann approves Melanchthon's statement: *"Christum cognoscere hoc est: beneficia ejus cognoscere, non ejus naturas et modos incarnationis intueri."* ("To know Christ is to know what he means for us instead of imagining what happened in the incarnation and how it happened.") For Bultmann, consequently, "every assertion about Christ is also an assertion about man and vice versa."[17] Or—and thus Bultmann justifies his reliance on the existential method—every assertion about Christ is also an assertion about authentic existence *and vice versa*. Philosophy and Christianity are concerned about the same thing: authentic existence. They are, therefore, agreed in what they call, respectively, inauthentic existence and sinful existence.

Are they also agreed in what they call authentic existence, on the one hand, and Christian existence, on the other? Here, Bultmann's thought appears to be ambiguous. He seems to say *yes* and *no.* Yes, in that authentic or Christian existence can be achieved only on the basis of a previous realization of one's inauthentic or sinful existence. Yes, because faith is not some supernatural or mysterious addition to man's self-understanding: it is the attitude of authentic man, just as love is, or should be, the natural, normal behavior of every man. Does this not eliminate Christ and what is peculiar to his rôle in Christian thought? No, argues Bultmann, because all that philosophy can state about authentic existence can only constitute an invocation of, an appeal to, God's activity; it can only announce God's redemptive activity; it can only announce the saving event accomplished in Christ.

In other words, the Christian understanding of man prior to faith, of man without Christ, must and can be demythologized, that is, stated in terms consonant with man's self-apprehension within any context. So also, the Christian understanding of man in Christ must and can be demythologized. The question is whether the transition from inauthentic to authentic depends on God's intervention and is inconceivable without the person and the work of Christ, without the Christ-event. Bultmann's cautious handling of this question indicates that the place accorded Christ in New Testament thought is indispensable and decisive for the transition to authentic existence. The Christ-event constitutes the only possibility of authentic existence. But the ambiguities of Bultmann's approach and its strict dependency on a phenomenological type of reflection which can be conducted with or without God, and especially with or without Christ, seem to indicate that this may very well be only a digression in the author's domestication of a post-Christian philosophical system. "It seems a fair criticism of Bultmann that he has concentrated on a fairly narrow intellectual front, and like the liberal modernist of fifty years ago, attempted to present the Christian faith in a form not likely to give offence to the modern outlook."[18] What is this modern outlook? Succinctly, it does not necessarily deny the existence of God, but at most it affirms his absence—as Heidegger has been reported to have said, by Gabriel Marcel in *L'Homme Problématique* and Macquarrie in *An Existentialist Philosophy*. One begins to wonder whether, as Tillich claims, "existentialism is the good luck of Christian theology" and whether "it has helped to rediscover the classical Christian interpretation of human existence."[19]

Both Bultmann and Tillich are agreed that philosophy cannot escape its religious background—at least this is true for existentialism; and that theology cannot escape its philosophical tools. Both consider opportune a correlation of these two quests for the meaning of human existence. Ultimately, both—Bultmann implicitly and Tillich explicitly—regard man as a being who asks questions. These questions must be correlated with their appropriate answers in such a way that the answer unlocks the labyrinth of the question. The answer must contain and reveal something

(2 2 4)

new, which the question did not suspect. As Tillich puts it, the substance of the answer must be
independent of the substance of the question.
Otherwise, the answer would not be a real answer.
It would merely rephrase the question affirma-
tively. Simultaneously, however, the *form* of the
answer cannot be independent of the form of the
question. Otherwise, it could not be understood,
or man would have to cease being a man in order
to understand it. Furthermore, man himself ultimately is a question, not an answer.[20] He himself
is the ultimate question of what the Christ-event
signifies.

This is all right, but it is equivocal: on the one
hand, before the act of faith and after it man is
both the same and no longer the same man; on the
other hand, it slightly glosses over the fact that
even if the substance of the answer must be different from that of the question, that substance
must be grounded in man's self-understanding
prior to the act of faith. The Scholastics of the
Middle Ages took for granted that reason would
normally lead to faith, unless it turned into unreason. The post-Scholastics knew better when
they realized that reason was indifferent: it could
lead to God and it could lead to the Devil. The
Reformers, because they recognized this autonomy of the reason, put all the emphasis on faith.
Now, the exponents of Christian existentialism
assume that the question of existence implies or
leads to the question of God.

It is, however, more legitimate to wonder

whether one may go from the first question to the second. Surely they can be correlated, but it does not follow that the principle of the correlation is included in the question of existence. Consequently, just as after the scientific impact it was realized that the universe both implied and did not imply a Supreme Being, so also the problem of man does and does not imply the problem of God. At best, Christian existentialism finds equivalences of a mythical and religious type of thought in a world which is basically hostile to that type, and has its foundation in a realm of thought governed by the immanentism of science and technology. Existentialist philosophy seeks the mythical possibilities of an unmythical, scientifically oriented self-consciousness. Existentialist theology naturally enough finds an ally in this philosophy. As Macquarrie has pointed out: "It is difficult to see how [Christian theology] can avoid being swallowed up in existentialist philosophy altogether. . . . The concepts of Christian existence could be taken over by existentialist philosophy without any reference to their origin in the cross and resurrection of Christ, and Christian theology would disappear as such."[21]

Somewhere, Tillich admits that it is conceivable that authentic existence in Christ may mean ceasing to be a Christian—which is what non-Christians have said in their argument in favor of authentic existence *tout court*. And Sartre has advocated that it entails forsaking Christ and God altogether; that it demands an atheistic humanism. Certainly, existentialism makes it impossible to identify God and man. No less certainly, this is so because God has already been eliminated. Thus, Sartre writes: "Every human reality is a passion in that it projects losing itself so as to found being and by the same stroke to constitute the In-itself which escapes contingency by being its own foundation, the *Ens causa sui,* which religions call God. Thus *the passion of man is the reverse of that of Christ,* for man loses himself as man in order that God may be born. But the idea of God is contradictory and we lose ourselves in vain. Man is a useless passion."[22]

In sum, existentialism is possible only in a world where God is dead or a luxury, and where Christianity is dead. It originates in the decay and death of Christianity. It presupposes the death of God, although in some of its aspects it may wish that God had not died. Or all this can be seen differently: in existentialism Christianity meets, in Carlyle's phrase, "not a torture death but a quiet euthanasia." Or again: existentialism transcribes in secular themes some aspects of man's sinful condition before God. It is, in a word, a transcription of the tragic condition of existence. But this tragedy is without heroes (as Sartre contends it should be) and without martyrs (as Kierkegaard complained it was). It is a tragedy without the tragic element.

Afterword

ARE WE living in a post-Christian era? The answer is manifold. It concerns not only the theological confines of Christianity, but the entire cultural complex in which the Western tradition has developed.

We live in a post-Christian era because Christianity has sunk into religiosity. No longer can this type of Christianity vitally define itself in terms of Biblical faith. Instead, it acquires the attributes of moralism, or those of a psychological and emotional welfare-state.

We live in a post-Christian era because modern culture is gradually losing the marks of that Christianity which brought it into being and shaped it. Whether from a national or an international perspective, Christianity has long since ceased to be coextensive with our culture, which day by day comes under extraneous influences.

And we live in a post-Christian era because tolerance has become religious syncretism, an

(228)

amalgam of beliefs and attitudes without content or backbone. Indeed, faith, hope, and love have nothing to do with these substitutes, no more than God with an idol, or my authentic self with the masks I am wearing.

One must ultimately come to terms with the reality here uncovered, even though partially and imperfectly. Kierkegaard in the nineteenth century complained about the tepid quality of the church and excoriated the Christianity of his day; and many others before him could be cited as taking a similar stand. Every age is post-Christian. But this has been true only *theologically* speaking; until modern times the formative tradition of Western culture has been continually imbued with the spirit of Christianity. Regardless of how approximately, our culture has been a variation on the translation of this spirit into the arts and the sciences, into a style of life. But the novelty, or tragedy, of our situation lies in the fact that our age is post-Christian both theologically and culturally.

In its dissolution by diffusion into the prevailing social climate, both popular and intellectual, Christianity has today reached a point of no return. Religiosity is the optical illusion which enables us to overlook the fact that, in Kierkegaard's words, "we no longer are capable of being Christians in the New Testament sense." Religiosity is apostasy from Christianity, just as our present culture is the betrayal of Christianity. In the tradition of Western culture "we have . . . reached the point of not knowing precisely what Christianity is."[1] Our age is post-Christian; but it is still religious.

The religiosity of our culture is not pagan, for we do not worship a stone, or an ox, or an insect. And it is not Christian, for we "worship under the name of God . . . a twaddler." This being so, "Christianity . . . does not exist," and God is dead —for nothing.

This, then, is the irony of the cultural tradition of Christianity: it has bequeathed us the idea of the death of God. This concept more and more evidently constitutes the foundation of our civilization, just as previously the idea of a Christian culture was founded on the presentness of God's reality. "To kill God is to become god oneself": This is the meaning of the transition from radical monotheism to radical immanentism which has taken place in Western culture. That is why, in Kierkegaard's view, immanentist religiosity is the greatest danger confronting man: it deifies man— the twaddler.

The ultimate absurdity of man's condition is in view. Once God is dead and man is deified, man is even more alone and estranged from himself than he ever was before.[2] He cannot even end his despair in divorcement from consciousness; suicide, the final act of cleavage from God, the extreme of the tragic element, offers no exit for him. And he cannot avenge himself upon God, since God died first. The deification of man, or *homo hominis deus* (man is the god of man), as Camus puts it, may yet show that man can avenge

(230)

himself upon man: *homo hominis lupus* (man is a wolf to man).

The radical immanentism of our cultural religiosity may be only provisional. In the light of Biblical thought, this immanentism can show that God dies as soon as he becomes a cultural accessory or a human ideal; that the finite cannot comprehend the infinite (*finitum non est capax infiniti*). From this point of view the death of God may be only a cultural phenomenon as though only our religio-cultural notion of God were dead. But this makes even more serious the question whether the transcendental view of man and his culture, as set forth in the Bible, has any chance of surviving the modern presupposition that God is dead.

The dilemma of radical immanentism is that it offers no resolution to man's predicament because, although it attempts to define man in terms of his relatedness to others, it can only project man as a god or a wolf to his fellow man. In Biblical thought, too, man is defined by his relatedness to others—"Thou shalt love thy neighbor as [though he were] thyself." But man, a finite being, neither defines nor comprehends—he is defined and comprehended by God the Infinite, the Wholly Other.

Good critique of alt.

Notes

PREFACE

1. Friedrich Nietzsche, *Thus Spake Zarathustra*, Part III, chap. 52, par. 2 in *The Philosophy of Nietzsche* (New York: Modern Library, 1954), p. 190.
2. *Ibid.*, Part II, chap. 24, p. 98.
3. *Ibid.*, Part IV, chap. 67, pp. 264-267.
4. Søren Kierkegaard, *The Point of View* (London: Oxford University Press, 1939), p. 70; and *Papirer*, X'A50.
5. Pascal, *Pensées*, No. 555.
6. Albert Camus, *The Rebel* (New York: Alfred A. Knopf, 1954), p. 204.
7. Henri de Lubac, *The Drama of Atheistic Humanism*, trans. Edith M. Riley (New York: Sheed and Ward, 1950).
8. Werner Elert, *The Christian Ethos*, trans. Carl J. Schindler (Philadelphia: Muhlenberg Press, 1957), p. 318.
9. *Op. cit.*, p. 273 (italics added).
10. Kenneth Boulding, "The Domestic Implications of Arms Control," *Daedalus* (Fall 1960), Vol. 89, No. 4, p. 849.
11. Jean-Paul Sartre, *Being and Nothingness*, trans. Hazel E. Barnes (New York: Philosophical Library, 1956), p. 412 and p. 70.

I. MODERN RELIGIOSITY and the CHRISTIAN TRADITION

1. Paul Tillich, *Systematic Theology* (Chicago: The University of Chicago Press, 1951), Vol. I, p. 3.
2. Rudolf Bultmann, *Theology of the New Testament*, trans. Kendrick Grobel (New York: Charles Scribner's Sons, 1954), Vol. I, p. 327.
3. Miguel de Unamuno, *l'Agonie du Christianisme*,

trans. by Jean Cassou from the unedited Spanish text (Paris: F. Rieder et Cie, 1925).

4. *Ibid.*, p. 19.

II. THE DISHABILITATION of the CHRISTIAN TRADITION

1. James Russell Lowell, essay on Thoreau cited by R. W. B. Lewis in *The American Adam: Innocence, Tragedy and Tradition in the Nineteenth Century* (Chicago: The University of Chicago Press, Phoenix Books), p. 23.

2. R. W. B. Lewis, *The American Adam.*

3. The reader will find a further discussion of this subject in Chapter VI.

4. H. Richard Niebuhr, *The Kingdom of God in America* (New York: Harper Torchbooks, 1959), p. 142.

5. *Ibid.*, p. 179.

6. *Ibid.*, pp. 178-179.

7. Perry Miller, *The American Puritans: Their Prose and Poetry* (Garden City, N.Y.: Doubleday Anchor Books, 1956), pp. 29-30.

8. Herbert W. Schneider, *The Puritan Mind* (Ann Arbor: The University of Michigan Press, Ann Arbor Paperbacks, 1958), p. 99.

9. *Ibid.*, p. 135.

10. R. W. B. Lewis, *op. cit.*, pp. 17, 19.

11. Josiah Strong, *The New Era, or The Coming Kingdom* (New York: Baker and Taylor, 1893), p. 256.

12. *Ibid.*, p. 257.

13. *Ibid.*, p. 240.

14. *Ibid.*, pp. 240-241.

15. *Ibid.*, p. 129.

16. Walter Rauschenbush, *The Social Principles of Jesus* (New York: Association Press, 1939), pp. 74 ff.

17. Max Lerner, *America as a Civilization: Life and Thought in the United States Today* (New York: Simon and Schuster, 1957), p. 705.

18. James Hastings Nichols, *History of Christianity, 1650-1950: Secularization of the West* (New York: The Ronald Press Company, 1956), p. 405.
19. Josiah Strong, *op. cit.*, p. 80.
20. *Ibid.*
21. J. H. Nichols, *op. cit.*, p. 330.
22. Josiah Strong, *op. cit.*, pp. 11, 12, 16. Cf. also *The Twentieth Century City* (New York: Baker and Taylor, 1898), chap. 6 and *The Challenge of the City*, 2nd ed. (New York: Eaton and Mains, 1907), pp. 179 ff.
23. *Ibid.*, p. 213.
24. Ernst Troeltsch, *The Social Teaching of the Christian Churches*, trans. Olive Wyon (London: George Allen and Unwin, Ltd.; New York: The Macmillan Company, 3d impression, 1950), vol. II, p. 992.
25. *Ibid.*
26. Ernst Troeltsch, *Christian Thought: Its History and Application*, ed. with an introduction and index by Baron F. von Hügel (New York: Meridian Books, 1957), p. 177.
27. Ernst Troeltsch, *De la possibilité d'un libre Christianisme*, p. 83.
28. *Ibid.*, p. 91.

III. MISBEGOTTEN REVIVAL

1. Samuel Beckett, *Waiting for Godot*, trans. from his original French text by the author (New York: Grove Press, 1954), p. 28.
2. *Ibid.*, p. 8.
3. Elio Vittorini, as reported in *Les Protestants et l'esthétique* (Paris: Le Semeur, 1949), p. 418.

IV. CHRISTIANITY, SECULARITY, and SECULARISM

1. Horton Davies, *A Mirror of the Ministry in Modern Novels* (New York: Oxford University Press, 1959), p. 39.

Notes

V. THE CASE for a NEW CHRISTIAN CULTURE

1. This short essay by T. S. Eliot has just been published together with *Notes Towards the Definition of Culture* under the common title of *Christianity and Culture* (New York: Harcourt, Brace and Company, a Harvest Book, n.d.).
2. Geneviève Ploquin, *Le Catholicisme* (Paris: Editions Buchet/Chastel, 1959), p. 146. (With *imprimatur*.)
3. Jacques Maritain, *Humanisme intégral: Problèmes temporels et spirituels d'une nouvelle Chrétienté* (Paris: Fernand Aubier, 1936). English trans. under the title *True Humanism* (London: Oxford University Press, 1938).
4. Cf. Maritain's *The Rights of Man and Natural Law,* trans. Doris C. Anson (New York: Charles Scribner's Sons, 1943).
5. Jacques Maritain, *Art and Scholasticism* (New York: Charles Scribner's Sons, 1938), p. 85; cf. also p. 223.
6. Jacques Maritain, *The Responsibility of the Artist* (New York: Charles Scribner's Sons, 1960).
7. Charles Frankel, *The Case for Modern Man* (New York: Harper and Brothers, 1955).
8. Jacques Maritain, *Sort de l'homme* (Neuchâtel: La Baconnière, 1943).

VI. PRESENT CULTURE and ITS CASE AGAINST CHRISTIANITY

1. "They wallow in the sublime—they lay it on thick." Georges Bernanos, *The Diary of a Country Priest* (New York: Doubleday Image Books, 1954), trans. Pamela Morris from *Le Journal d'un Curé de campagne* (Paris: Plon, 1936).
2. Graham Greene, *The Power and the Glory* (New

York: Viking Press, Compass Books, 1958). Previously published in America under the title *The Labyrinthine Ways*.

3. Pamela Morris's translation. Wherever no such mention is made, I have used my own translations from the French.
4. Gilbert Cesbron, *Les Saints vont en enfer* (Paris: Robert Laffont, 1952).
5. François Mauriac, *The Lamb,* trans. Gerard Hopkins (New York: Farrar, Straus and Cudahy, 1955).
6. Archibald MacLeish, *J.B.* (Boston: Houghton Mifflin Company, 1958).
7. W. H. Auden, in *The New York Times Book Review,* December 16, 1945.
8. Cf. Chapter I.

VII. CULTURAL INCAPACITY for GOD: THE ABSENCE of GOD'S REALITY

1. Charles Williams, *The Descent of the Dove* (New York: Meridian Books, 1956), p. 83.
2. Herbert W. Schneider, *The Puritan Mind* (Ann Arbor: The University of Michigan Press, Ann Arbor Paperbacks, 1958).
3. Ludwig Feuerbach, *The Essence of Christianity,* trans. from the German by George Eliot (New York: Harper Torchbooks, 1957), p. 29.
4. Montesquieu, *De l'esprit des lois,* Vol. XXIV, chap. 3, *Œuvres complètes de Montesquieu* (Paris: Firmin Didot, 1870), p. 407.
5. John Calvin, *Institutes of the Christian Religion,* trans. John Allen (Philadelphia: Presbyterian Board of Christian Education, 1935), Book I, chap. 1, secs. 1, 2.
6. Hanns Lilje, *The New York Times,* March 11, 1960, p. 2.

7. *The Village Voice*, February 17, 1960.
8. Christopher Dawson, *The Historic Reality of Christian Culture* (New York: Harper and Brothers, 1960), pp. 29-30.
9. Karl Jaspers, *The Origin and Goal of History* (New Haven: Yale University Press, 1953).
10. Pitirim Sorokin, *The Crisis of Our Age* (New York: E. P. Dutton and Company, 1942), p. 26.
11. Arnold Toynbee, *Civilization on Trial* (New York: Oxford University Press, 1948), pp. 244-245.
12. *Ibid.*, p. 240.
13. Malcolm L. Diamond, *Martin Buber: Jewish Existentialist* (New York: Oxford University Press, 1960).
14. Christopher Dawson, *op. cit.*, p. 17.
15. *Ibid.*, p. 46.
16. T. S. Eliot, *Christianity and Culture* (New York: Harcourt, Brace and Company, Harvest Book, n.d.) p. 10.
17. *Ibid.*, p. 19.
18. Ernst Troeltsch, *Christian Thought: Its History and Application*, ed. with an introduction and index by Baron F. von Hügel (New York: Meridian Books, 1957), p. 54.
19. C. P. Cavafy, "The City," trans. Lawrence Durrell in *Justine* (New York: E. P. Dutton and Co., 1957), p. 252.

VIII. CULTURAL DISAVOWAL of GOD: THE REALITY of GOD'S ABSENCE

1. Reinhold Niebuhr, *An Interpretation of Christian Ethics* (New York: Harper and Brothers, 1935), p. 26.
2. Carl Michalson, "The Real Presence of the Hidden God," in Paul Ramsey (ed.), *Faith and Ethics: The Theology of H. Richard Niebuhr* (New York: Harper and Brothers, 1957), p. 257.

3. James Hastings Nichols, *History of Christianity, 1650-1950: Secularization of the West* (New York: The Ronald Press Company, 1956), pp. 270-271.
4. H. Richard Niebuhr, *Christ and Culture* (New York: Harper and Brothers, 1951), pp. 110-111.
5. Jean-Paul Sartre, "Les Mouches," *Théâtre* (Paris: Gallimard, 1947), I, 99-100.

IX. THE LEGACY of CHRISTIANITY:
ITS SELF-INVALIDATION

1. Norman Vincent Peale, *The Power of Positive Thinking* (New York: Prentice-Hall, 1953), pp. 63-64. Mr. Peale even articulates business religiosity in a quasi-credal slogan: "Prayerize! Picturize! Actualize!" *Ibid.*, pp. 55 ff.
2. L. Schneider, and S. M. Dornbusch, *Popular Religion: Inspirational Books in America* (Chicago: The University of Chicago Press, 1958), p. 70.
3. *Ibid.*, p. 144.
4. Martin E. Marty, *The New Shape of American Religion* (New York: Harper and Brothers, 1959), p. 73.
5. ". . . it is with God we must be the most careful; for He makes such a powerful appeal to what is *lowest* in human nature . . ." Lawrence Durrell, *Justine* (New York: E. P. Dutton and Co., 1957), p. 140.
6. Søren Kierkegaard, *Attack Upon Christendom*, trans. Walter Lowrie (Boston: The Beacon Press, 1956), p. 2.
7. Søren Kierkegaard, *Concluding Unscientific Postscript*, trans. David Swenson (completed after his death by Walter Lowrie) (Princeton: Princeton University Press, 1941), p. 342.
8. *Ibid.*, p. 424.
9. Paul Tillich, *Systematic Theology* (Chicago: The University of Chicago Press, 1951).

10. Søren Kierkegaard, *The Sickness Unto Death,* trans. Walter Lowrie (Garden City: Doubleday Anchor Books, 1954), pp. 150, 151.
11. Jean-Paul Sartre, *The Reprieve,* trans. Eric Sutton (New York: Alfred A. Knopf, 1947), p. 407.
12. John Macquarrie, *An Existentialist Theology* (London: S. C. M. Press, 1955), p. 240.
13. Jean-Paul Sartre, *L'Etre et le Néant* (Paris: Gallimard, 1943), p. 122.
14. Rudolf Bultmann, "New Testament and Mythology," in Hans Werner Bartsch (ed.), *Kerygma and Myth,* trans. Reginald H. Fuller (London: S.P.C.K., 1957).
15. Rudolf Bultmann, *Theology of the New Testament,* trans. Kendrick Grobel (New York: Charles Scribner's Sons, 1954), Vol. I, p. 190.
16. *Ibid.,* p. 191.
17. *Ibid.*
18. John Macquarrie, *op. cit.,* p. 246.
19. Paul Tillich, *Systematic Theology* (Chicago: The University of Chicago Press, 1957), Vol. II, p. 27.
20. *Ibid.,* p. 137.
21. John Macquarrie, *op. cit.,* p. 240.
22. Jean-Paul Sartre, *Being and Nothingness,* trans. Hazel E. Barnes (New York: Philosophical Library, 1956), p. 615 (italics added.)

AFTERWORD

1. Søren Kierkegaard, *Attack Upon Christendom,* trans. Walter Lowrie (Boston: The Beacon Press, 1956).
2. Jean-Paul Sartre, *Le Diable et le Bon Dieu* (Paris: Gallimard, 1951).

Suggestions for Further Reading

AQUINAS, THOMAS. *Basic Writings.* New York: Random House, 1945.

AUDEN, W. H. *The Collected Poetry of W. H. Auden.* New York: Random House, 1945.

AUERBACH, ERICH. *Mimesis.* Princeton, N.J.: Princeton University Press, 1953; New York: Doubleday Anchor Books, 1957.

AUGUSTINE, SAINT. *The Basic Writings of St. Augustine.* New York: Random House, 1948.

BACON, FRANCIS. *Selected Writings of Francis Bacon.* New York: Modern Library, 1955.

BARTH, KARL. *Church Dogmatics* (2nd impression). Edinburgh: T. & T. Clark, 1949.

———. *The Faith of the Church.* New York: Meridian, 1958.

———. *Protestant Thought from Rousseau to Ritschl.* New York: Harper, 1959.

BARTSCH, H. W. (ed.). *Kerygma and Myth.* Translated by REGINALD FULLER. New York: Macmillan, 1954.

BATES, E. S. *American Religion: Its Religious, Political, and Economic Foundations.* New York: W. W. Norton, 1940.

BAUMER, F. L. *Religion and the Rise of Scepticism.* New York: Harcourt, Brace, 1960.

Suggestions for Further Reading

BECKETT, SAMUEL. *Waiting for Godot.* New York: Grove Press, 1954; Grove Press Evergreen Book, 1956.

BENDA, JULIEN. *La trahison des clercs.* Paris: Grasset, 1927; *The Betrayal of the Intellectuals,* Boston: Beacon Paperback, 1955.

BERNANOS, GEORGES. *Journal d'un Curé de campagne.* Paris: Plon, 1936; *Diary of a Country Priest,* New York: Doubleday Image Book, 1954.

BEVAN, EDWYN. *Symbolism and Belief.* London: Allen and Unwin, 1938; Boston: Beacon Paperback, 1957.

BLANCHET, ANDRÉ. *Le Prêtre dans le roman d'aujourd'hui.* Paris: Desclée de Brouwer, 1955.

BONHOEFFER, D. *The Cost of Discipleship.* London: S. C. M. Press, 1954.

————. *Ethics.* New York: Macmillan, 1955.

BRÉMOND, HENRI. *Prière et poésie.* Paris: Grasset, 1926.

BRINTON, CRANE. *The Shaping of the Modern Mind.* New York: New American Library Mentor Book, 1953.

BRUNNER, EMIL. *Christianity and Civilization.* New York: Scribner's, 1949.

BUBER, MARTIN. *I and Thou.* New York: Scribner's, 1957; Scribner's Paperback, 1958.

BULTMANN, RUDOLF. *Existence and Faith.* New York: Meridian, 1960.

————. *Jesus Christ and Mythology.* New York: Scribner's, 1958.

————. *Jesus and the Word.* New York and London: Scribner's, 1934; New York: Scribner's Paperback, 1960.

————. *The Presence of Eternity: History and Eschatology.* New York: Harper, 1957.

————. *Primitive Christianity in Its Contemporary Setting.* New York: Meridian, 1956.

————. *Theology of the New Testament.* New York: Scribner's, 1951-55.

BURTT, E. A. *English Philosophers from Bacon to Mill.* New York: Modern Library, 1939.

————. *The Metaphysical Foundations of Modern Physical Science.* New York: Harcourt, Brace, 1925.

————. *Types of Religious Philosophy.* New York: Harper, 1951.

BUTTERFIELD, HERBERT. *The Origins of Modern Science.* New York: Macmillan, 1951; Macmillan Paperback, 1960.

CALVIN, JOHN. *Institutes of the Christian Religion.* Philadelphia: Presbyterian Board of Christian Education, 1935; Grand Rapids: Wm. B. Eerdmans Publishing Co. (paperback), 1953.

CAMUS, ALBERT. *The Rebel.* New York: Knopf, 1954; Knopf Vintage Book, 1956.

CASSIRER, ERNST. *An Essay on Man.* New York: Doubleday Anchor Book, 1956.

CESBRON, GILBERT. *Les Saints vont en enfer.* Paris: Laffont, 1952.

COCHRANE, CHARLES N. *Christianity and Classical Culture.* New York: Oxford University Press, 1944; Oxford Galaxy Book, 1957.

D'ARCY, M. C. *The Meaning and Matter of History.* New York: Farrar, Straus & Cudahy, 1959; Meridian Books, 1960.

DARWIN, CHARLES. *On the Origin of Species.* New York: Appleton-Century-Crofts, 1877; New American Library, 1958.

DAVIES, HORTON. *A Mirror of the Ministry in Modern Novels.* New York: Oxford University Press, 1959.

DAWSON, CHRISTOPHER. *Enquiries into Religion and Culture.* New York: Sheed and Ward, 1936.

Suggestions for Further Reading

———. *The Historic Reality of Christian Culture.* New York: Harper, 1960.

———. *Religion and Culture.* London: Sheed and Ward, 1948; New York: Meridian, 1958.

———. *Religion and the Rise of Western Culture.* London: Sheed and Ward, 1950; New York: Doubleday Image Book, 1958.

DESCARTES, RENÉ. *Selections.* New York: Scribner's 1928; Scribner's Paperback, 1955.

DIAMOND, M. L. *Martin Buber: Jewish Existentialist.* New York: Oxford University Press, 1960.

DILTHEY, WILHELM. *Weltanschauung und Analyse des Menschen seit Renaissance und Reformation.* Leipzig and Berlin: Teubner, 1914.

DUNBAR, H. F. *Symbolism in Medieval Thought and Its Consummation in "The Divine Comedy."* New Haven, Conn.: Yale University Press, 1929.

DURRELL, LAWRENCE. *Justine.* New York: Dutton, 1957.

ECKHARDT, A. ROY. *The Surge of Piety in America: An Appraisal.* New York: Association Press, 1958.

EDWARDS, JONATHAN. *Freedom of the Will.* New Haven, Conn.: Yale University Press, 1957.

———. *The Nature of True Virtue.* Ann Arbor, Mich.: Ann Arbor Paperback, 1960.

ELIADE, MIRCEA. *Birth and Rebirth.* New York: Harper, 1958.

———. *Cosmos and History: The Myth of the Eternal Return.* New York: Harper Torchbook, 1959.

———. *The Sacred and the Profane.* New York: Harcourt, Brace, 1959.

ELIOT, T. S. *Christianity and Culture.* New York: Harcourt, Brace, Harvest Book, 1960.

ELLUL, JACQUES. *La technique ou l'enjeu du siècle.* Paris: Colin, 1954.

ERASMUS, DESIDERIUS. *The Praise of Folly.* Ann Arbor, Mich.: Ann Arbor Paperback, 1960.

FEUERBACH, LUDWIG. *The Essence of Christianity.* New York: Harper Torchbook, 1957.

FREMANTLE, ANNE. *The Papal Encyclicals in Their Historical Context.* New York: New American Library Mentor Book, 1956.

FREUD, SIGMUND. *The Future of an Illusion.* New York: Doubleday Anchor Book, 1957.

FROMM, ERICH. *Man for Himself.* New York: Rinehart, 1947.

———. *Psychoanalysis and Religion.* New Haven, Conn.: Yale University Press, 1950; Yale University Press Paperbound, 1959.

GRAHAM, BILLY. *Peace with God.* New York: Pocket Books Permabook, 1960.

GREENE, GRAHAM. *The Power and the Glory.* New York: Viking, 1940; Viking Compass Book, 1958.

HARNACK, ADOLF. *What Is Christianity?* New York: Harper Torchbook, 1957.

HAUSER, ARNOLD. *The Social History of Art.* New York: Knopf Vintage Book, 1957.

HEGEL, G. W. F. *Early Theological Writings.* Chicago: University of Chicago Press, 1948.

HELLER, ERICH. *The Disinherited Mind.* New York: Farrar, Straus & Cudahy, 1957; Meridian, 1959.

HOLL, KARL. *The Cultural Significance of the Reformation.* New York: Meridian, 1959.

HOPPER, S. R. *Spiritual Problems in Contemporary Literature.* New York: Harper, 1952; Harper Torchbook, 1957.

HUGHES, PHILIP. *A Popular History of the Catholic Church.* New York: Macmillan, 1953; Doubleday Image Book, 1954.

HUME, DAVID. *Selections.* New York: Scribner's, 1927; Scribner's Paperback, 1955.

Suggestions for Further Reading

JAMES, WILLIAM. *Varieties of Religious Experience.* New York: Modern Library, 1936; Doubleday Dolphin Book, 1960.

JASPERS, KARL. *Man in the Modern Age.* New York: Holt, 1933; Doubleday Anchor Book, 1957.

———. *The Origin and Goal of History.* New Haven: Yale University Press, 1953.

———. *The Perennial Scope of Philosophy.* New York: Philosophical Library, 1949.

JASPERS, KARL, and BULTMANN, RUDOLF. *Myth and Christianity: An Inquiry into the Possibility of Religion without Myth.* New York: Noonday, 1958.

JUNG, CARL GUSTAV. *Psychology and Religion.* New York: Pantheon, 1958; New Haven, Conn.: Yale University Press Paperbound, 1960.

KANT, IMMANUEL. *Selections.* New York: Scribner's, 1929; Scribner's Paperback, 1957.

KAUFMANN, WALTER. *Critique of Religion and Philosophy.* New York: Harper, 1958.

KAUFMANN, WALTER (ed.). *Existentialism from Dostoevsky to Sartre.* New York: Meridian, 1956.

KEGLEY, C. W., and BRETALL, R. W. (eds.). *The Theology of Paul Tillich.* New York: Macmillan, 1952.

KIERKEGAARD, SØREN. *Attack Upon Christendom.* Boston: Beacon Paperback, 1956.

———. *Concluding Unscientific Postscript.* Princeton, N. J.: Princeton University Press, 1941.

———. *Fear and Trembling* and *The Sickness unto Death.* New York: Doubleday Anchor Book, 1954.

KRONER, RICHARD. *Culture and Faith.* Chicago: University of Chicago Press, 1951.

KRUTCH, JOSEPH WOOD. *The Modern Temper.* New York: Harcourt, Brace, Harvest Book, 1956.

LACROIX, JEAN. *Le sens de l'athéisme moderne.* Tournai: Casterman, 1959.

LATOURETTE, K. S. *The Nineteenth Century: Background and the Roman Catholic Phase.* (*Christianity in a Revolutionary Age,* Vol. I.) New York: Harper, 1958.

LECOMTE DU NOÜY, P. *Human Destiny.* New York: New American Library Signet Book, 1949.

LEIBRECHT, W. (ed.). *Religion and Culture: Essays in Honor of Paul Tillich.* New York: Harper, 1959.

LERNER, MAX. *America as a Civilization.* New York: Simon and Schuster, 1957; Simon and Schuster Paperback, 1960.

LEWIS, R. W. B. *The American Adam: Innocence, Tragedy, and Tradition in the Nineteenth Century.* Chicago: University of Chicago Press, 1955; University of Chicago Press Phoenix Book, 1959.

LIEBMAN, JOSHUA. *Peace of Mind.* New York: Simon and Schuster, 1949.

LOCKE, JOHN. *The Reasonableness of Christianity.* Stanford, Calif.: Stanford University Press, 1958.

LUTHER, MARTIN. *Works of Martin Luther.* Philadelphia: Muhlenberg, 1915–1932.

MACLEISH, ARCHIBALD. *J. B.* Boston: Houghton Mifflin, 1958.

MACQUARRIE, JOHN. *An Existentialist Theology.* London: S. C. M. Press, 1955.

MÂLE, EMILE. *Religious Art from the Twelfth to the Eighteenth Century.* New York: Pantheon, 1949; Noonday Press, 1958.

MALINOWSKI, BRONISLAW. *Magic, Science and Religion.* New York: Doubleday Anchor Book, 1955.

MALRAUX, ANDRÉ. *The Metamorphosis of the Gods.* New York: Doubleday, 1960.

———. *The Voices of Silence.* New York: Doubleday, 1953.

(247)

MARCEL, GABRIEL. *L'homme problématique*. Paris: Aubier, 1955.

——. *The Philosophy of Existence*. New York: Philosophical Library, 1949.

MARITAIN, JACQUES. *Art and Faith* (letters between Jacques Maritain and Jean Cocteau). New York: Philosophical Library, 1948.

——. *Art and Scholasticism*. New York: Scribner's, 1938.

——. *Creative Intuition in Art and Poetry*. New York: Meridian, 1955.

——. *Le crépuscule de la civilisation*. Montréal: L'Arbre, 1941.

——. *Humanisme intégral: problèmes temporels et spirituels d'une nouvelle Chrétienté*. Paris: Aubier, 1936; *True Humanism*, various editions.

——. *Religion et culture* (2d ed.). Paris: Desclée de Brouwer, 1930.

——. *The Responsibility of the Artist*. New York: Scribner's, 1960.

——. *Sort de l'homme*. Neuchâtel, Switzerland: La Baconnière, 1943.

MARITAIN, J., and MARITAIN, R. *Situation de la poésie*. Paris: Desclée de Brouwer, 1938.

MARTY, M. E. *The New Shape of American Religion*. New York: Harper, 1959.

MASCALL, E. L. *Christian Theology and Natural Science*. New York: Ronald Press, 1957.

MAURIAC, FRANÇOIS. *The Lamb*. New York: Farrar, Straus & Cudahy, 1955.

MAURIS, EDOUARD, *et al*. *L'athéisme contemporain*. Genève: Labor et Fides, n.d.

MAY, ROLLO (ed.). *Symbolism in Religion and Literature*. New York: Braziller, 1960.

MEAD, MARGARET (ed.). *Cultural Patterns and Tech-*

nical Change. Paris: UNESCO, 1953; New York: New American Library, 1955.

MICHALSON, CARL (ed.). *Christianity and the Existentialists*. New York: Scribner's, 1958.

MIEGGE, GIOVANNI. *Christian Affirmations in a Secular Age*. New York: Oxford University Press, 1958.

MILLER, PERRY. *The New England Mind*. New York: Macmillan, 1939.

———. *Orthodoxy in Massachusetts*. Boston: Beacon Paperback, 1959.

MILLER, PERRY (ed.). *The American Puritans*. New York: Doubleday Anchor Book, 1956.

———. *The Golden Age of American Literature*. New York: Braziller, 1959.

MONTESQUIEU, BARON DE. *Œuvres complètes*. Paris: Garnier, 1875-79.

MURRAY, HENRY A. (ed.). *Myth and Mythmaking*. New York: Braziller, 1960.

NICHOLS, JAMES H. *History of Christianity 1650–1950: Secularization of the West*. New York: Ronald Press, 1956.

NIEBUHR, H. RICHARD. *Christ and Culture*. New York: Harper, 1951; Harper Torchbook, 1956.

———. *The Kingdom of God in America*. New York: Harper Torchbook, 1959.

———. *Radical Monotheism and Western Culture*. New York: Harper, 1960.

NIEBUHR, REINHOLD. *Faith and History*. New York: Harper, 1947.

———. *The Nature and Destiny of Man*. New York: Scribner's, 1941.

NIETZSCHE, FRIEDRICH. *Thus Spake Zarathustra*. New York: Modern Library, 1937.

ORTEGA Y GASSET, JOSÉ. *The Dehumanization of Art*. New York: Doubleday Anchor Book, 1956.

————. *The Revolt of the Masses.* New York: New American Library Mentor Book, 1950.

OTTO, RUDOLF. *The Idea of the Holy* (2d ed.). London: Oxford University Press, 1950; New York: Oxford Galaxy Book, 1958.

PARKES, HENRY B. *Gods and Men: The Origins of Western Culture.* New York: Knopf, 1959.

PASCAL, BLAISE. *Pensées* and *The Provincial Letters.* New York: Modern Library, 1941.

PEALE, NORMAN VINCENT. *The Power of Positive Thinking.* Englewood Cliffs, N.J.: Prentice-Hall, 1953.

PHILLIPS, J. B. *God Our Contemporary.* New York: Macmillan, 1960; Macmillan Paperback, 1960.

PLOQUIN, GENEVIÈVE. *Le Catholicisme.* Paris: Buchet/Chastel, 1959.

RAMSEY, PAUL (ed.). *Faith and Ethics.* New York: Harper, 1957.

RAUSCHENBUSCH, W. *Christianizing the Social Order.* New York: Macmillan, 1912.

————. *A Theology for the Social Gospel.* New York: Macmillan, 1919.

ROBERTS, DAVID E. *Existentialism and Religious Belief.* New York: Oxford University Press, 1947; Oxford Galaxy Book, 1960.

ROUGEMONT, DENIS DE. *L'aventure occidentale de l'homme.* Paris: Albin Michel, 1957; New York: Harper, 1957.

ROYCE, JOSIAH. *The Spirit of Modern Philosophy.* Boston: Houghton Mifflin, 1892.

RUSSELL, BERTRAND. *Religion and Science.* New York: Holt, 1935; Galaxy Books, 1961.

SANTAYANA, GEORGE. *Poetry and Religion.* New York: Harper Torchbook, 1957.

————. *Reason in Religion.* New York: Scribner's, 1915.

SARTRE, JEAN-PAUL. *Being and Nothingness.* New York: Philosophical Library, 1956.

————. *The Reprieve.* New York: Knopf, 1947; Bantam Books, 1960.

————. *What Is Literature?* New York: Philosophical Library, 1949.

SCHLEIERMACHER, FRIEDRICH. *The Christian Faith.* Edinburgh: T. & T. Clark, 1948; Naperville, Ill.: Alec R. Allenson, 1958.

————. *On Religion: Speeches to Its Cultured Despisers.* New York: Ungar, 1955; Harper Torchbook, 1958.

SCHNEIDER, H. W. *The Puritan Mind.* Ann Arbor, Mich.: Ann Arbor Paperback, 1958.

————. *Religion in Twentieth-Century America.* Cambridge, Mass.: Harvard University Press, 1952.

SCHNEIDER, L., and DORNBUSCH, S. M. *Popular Religion.* Chicago: University of Chicago Press, 1958.

SCHWEITZER, ALBERT. *The Philosophy of Civilization.* New York: Macmillan Paperback, 1960.

SCOTT, N. A., JR. (ed.). *The Tragic Vision and the Christian Faith.* New York: Association, 1957.

SHEEN, FULTON. *Peace of Soul.* New York: McGraw-Hill, 1949; Doubleday Image Book, 1954.

SIMON, PIERRE-HENRI. *La littérature du péché et de la grâce.* Paris: Fayard, 1957.

SOROKIN, PITIRIM A. *The Crisis of Our Age.* New York: Dutton, 1942; Dutton Everyman Paperback, 1957.

STACE, W. T. *Religion and the Modern Mind.* Philadelphia: Lippincott, 1952; Lippincott Keystone Book, 1960.

STRONG, JOSIAH. *Expansion under New World Conditions.* New York: Baker and Taylor, 1900.

Suggestions for Further Reading

————. *The New Era, or The Coming Kingdom.* New York: Baker and Taylor, 1893.

SWEET, W. W. *The Story of Religion in America.* New York: Harper, 1939.

SZCZESNY, GERHARD. *The Future of Unbelief.* New York: Braziller, 1961.

TEILHARD DE CHARDIN, P. *The Divine Milieu.* New York: Harper, 1960.

————. *The Phenomenon of Man.* New York: Harper, 1959.

THOMAS, GEORGE (ed.). *The Vitality of the Christian Tradition.* New York: Harper, 1944.

TILLICH, PAUL. *The Protestant Era.* Chicago: University of Chicago Press, 1948.

————. *The Religious Situation.* New York: Holt, 1932; Meridian, 1956.

————. *Systematic Theology.* 2 vols. Chicago: University of Chicago Press, 1951, 1957.

————. *Theology of Culture.* New York: Oxford University Press, 1959.

TOYNBEE, ARNOLD J. *Christianity among the World Religions.* New York: Scribner's, 1957.

————. *Civilization on Trial* and *The World and the West.* New York: Meridian, 1958.

————. *A Study of History.* Abridgment by D. C. SOMERVELL. New York and London: Oxford University Press, 1947.

TRINTERUD, L. J. *The Forming of an American Tradition.* Philadelphia: Westminster, 1949.

TROELTSCH, E. *Christian Thought.* New York: Meridian, 1957.

————. *Protestantism and Progress.* Boston: Beacon Paperback, 1958.

————. *The Social Teaching of the Christian Churches.*

New York: Macmillan, 1950; Harper Torchbook (2 vols.), 1960.

TROTSKY, LEON. *Literature and Revolution.* New York: International, 1925; Ann Arbor, Mich.: Ann Arbor Paperback, 1960.

UNAMUNO, MIGUEL DE. *L'agonie du Christianisme.* Paris: Rieder, 1925.

URBAN, W. M. *Language and Reality.* New York: Macmillan, 1939.

VAN DUSEN, H. P. (ed.). *The Christian Answer.* New York: Scribner's, 1946.

VANN, GERALD, O.P. *The Water and the Fire.* New York: Sheed and Ward, 1954.

VISSER 'T HOOFT, W. A. *Rembrandt and the Gospel.* Philadelphia: Westminster, 1958; New York: Meridian, 1960.

WALKER, WILLISTON. *A History of the Christian Church.* New York: Scribner's, 1959.

WALSH, CHAD. *Early Christians of the Twenty-first Century.* New York: Harper, 1949.

WEIDLE, WLADIMIR. *The Dilemma of the Arts.* London: S. C. M. Press, 1948.

WHITEHEAD, ALFRED NORTH. *Science and the Modern World.* New York: New American Library Mentor Book, 1952.

———. *Symbolism: Its Meaning and Effect.* Cambridge, England: Cambridge University Press, 1928; New York: G. P. Putnam's Capricorn Book, 1959.

WILDER, AMOS H. *Modern Poetry and the Christian Tradition.* New York: Scribner's, 1952.

———. *Theology and Modern Literature.* Cambridge, Mass.: Harvard University Press, 1958.

WILLIAMS, CHARLES. *The Descent of the Dove.* New York: Meridian, 1956.